A FAREWELL TO ARMS

Ernest Hemingway

SPARK PUBLISHING

SPARKNOTES is a registered trademark of SparkNotes LLC

Spark Publishing
A Division of Barnes & Noble
120 Fifth Avenue
New York, NY 10011
www.sparknotes.com

ISBN-13: 978-1-4114-0495-3
ISBN-10: 1-4114-0495-5

Please submit changes or report errors to www.sparknotes.com/errors.

Printed in the United States.

10 9 8 7 6 5 4 3 2

CONTENTS

CONTEXT

ERNEST HEMINGWAY WAS BORN in Oak Park, Illinois, in the summer of 1899. He later portrayed his middle-class parents rather harshly, condemning them for their conventional morality and values. As a young man, he left home to become a newspaper writer in Kansas City. Early in 1918, he joined the Italian Red Cross and served as an ambulance driver in Italy during World War I, in which the Italians allied with the British, French, and Americans against Germany and Austria-Hungary. During his time abroad, Hemingway had two experiences that affected him profoundly and that would later inspire one of his most celebrated novels, *A Farewell to Arms*. The first occurred on July 8, 1918, when a trench mortar shell struck him while he crouched beyond the front lines with three Italian soldiers. Though Hemingway embellished the story over the years, it is certain that he was transferred to a hospital in Milan, where he fell in love with a Red Cross nurse named Agnes von Kurowsky. Scholars are divided over Agnes's role in Hemingway's life and writing, but there is little doubt that his relationship with her informed the relationship between Lieutenant Henry and Catherine Barkley in *A Farewell to Arms*.

After his recovery, Hemingway spent several years as a reporter, during which time he honed the clear, concise, and emotionally evocative writing style that generations of authors after him would imitate. In September 1921, he married his first of four wives and settled in Paris, where he made valuable connections with American expatriate writers including Gertrude Stein and Ezra Pound. Hemingway's landmark collection of stories, *In Our Time,* introduced Nick Adams, one of the author's favorite protagonists, whose difficult road from youth into maturity he chronicled. Hemingway's reputation as a writer, however, was most firmly established by the publication of *The Sun Also Rises* in 1926 and *A Farewell to Arms* in 1929.

Critics generally agree that *A Farewell to Arms* is Hemingway's most accomplished novel. It offers powerful descriptions of life during and immediately following World War I and brilliantly maps the psychological complexities of its characters using a revolutionary, pared-down prose style. Furthermore, the novel, like much of Hemingway's writing during what were to be his golden years, helped to establish the author's myth of himself as a master of many trades: writing, soldiering, boxing, bullfighting, big-game hunting.

Hemingway was skilled, to a greater or lesser extent, in each of these arts, but most critics maintain that his writing fizzled after World War II, when his physical and mental health declined. Despite fantastic bouts of depression, Hemingway did muster enough energy to write *The Old Man and the Sea,* one of his most beloved stories, in 1952. This novella earned him a Pulitzer Prize, and three years later Hemingway was awarded the Nobel Prize in Literature. Still, not even these accolades could soothe the devastating effects of a lifetime of debilitating depression. On July 2, 1961, Hemingway killed himself in his home in Ketchum, Idaho.

PLOT OVERVIEW

L IEUTENANT FREDERIC HENRY is a young American ambulance driver serving in the Italian army during World
War I. At the beginning of the novel, the war is winding
down with the onset of winter, and Henry arranges to
tour Italy. The following spring, upon his return to the
front, Henry meets Catherine Barkley, an English nurse's aide at the
nearby British hospital and the love interest of his friend Rinaldi.
Rinaldi, however, quickly fades from the picture as Catherine and
Henry become involved in an elaborate game of seduction. Grieving
the recent death of her fiancé, Catherine longs for love so deeply that
she will settle for the illusion of it. Her passion, even though pre-
tended, wakens a desire for emotional interaction in Henry, whom
the war has left coolly detached and numb.

When Henry is wounded on the battlefield, he is brought to a
hospital in Milan to recover. Several doctors recommend that he
stay in bed for six months and then undergo a necessary operation
on his knee. Unable to accept such a long period of recovery, Henry
finds a bold, garrulous surgeon named Dr. Valentini who agrees
to operate immediately. Henry learns happily that Catherine has
been transferred to Milan and begins his recuperation under her
care. During the following months, his relationship with Catherine
intensifies. No longer simply a game in which they exchange empty
promises and playful kisses, their love becomes powerful and real.
As the lines between scripted and genuine emotions begin to blur,
Henry and Catherine become tangled in their love for each other.

Once Henry's damaged leg has healed, the army grants him three
weeks convalescence leave, after which he is scheduled to return to
the front. He tries to plan a trip with Catherine, who reveals to him
that she is pregnant. The following day, Henry is diagnosed with
jaundice, and Miss Van Campen, the superintendent of the hospital,
accuses him of bringing the disease on himself through excessive
drinking. Believing Henry's illness to be an attempt to avoid his duty
as a serviceman, Miss Van Campen has Henry's leave revoked, and
he is sent to the front once the jaundice has cleared. As they part,
Catherine and Henry pledge their mutual devotion.

Henry travels to the front, where Italian forces are losing ground
and manpower daily. Soon after Henry's arrival, a bombardment

begins. When word comes that German troops are breaking through the Italian lines, the Allied forces prepare to retreat. Henry leads his team of ambulance drivers into the great column of evacuating troops. The men pick up two engineering sergeants and two frightened young girls on their way. Henry and his drivers then decide to leave the column and take secondary roads, which they assume will be faster. When one of their vehicles bogs down in the mud, Henry orders the two engineers to help in the effort to free the vehicle. When they refuse, he shoots one of them. The drivers continue in the other trucks until they get stuck again. They send off the young girls and continue on foot toward Udine. As they march, one of the drivers is shot dead by the easily frightened rear guard of the Italian army. Another driver marches off to surrender himself, while Henry and the remaining driver seek refuge at a farmhouse. When they rejoin the retreat the following day, chaos has broken out: soldiers, angered by the Italian defeat, pull commanding officers from the melee and execute them on sight. The battle police seize Henry, who, at a crucial moment, breaks away and dives into the river. After swimming a safe distance downstream, Henry boards a train bound for Milan. He hides beneath a tarp that covers stockpiled artillery, thinking that his obligations to the war effort are over and dreaming of his return to Catherine.

Henry reunites with Catherine in the town of Stresa. From there, the two escape to safety in Switzerland, rowing all night in a tiny borrowed boat. They settle happily in a lovely alpine town called Montreux and agree to put the war behind them forever. Although Henry is sometimes plagued by guilt for abandoning the men on the front, the two succeed in living a beautiful, peaceful life. When spring arrives, the couple moves to Lausanne so that they can be closer to the hospital. Early one morning, Catherine goes into labor. The delivery is exceptionally painful and complicated. Catherine delivers a stillborn baby boy and, later that night, dies of a hemorrhage. Henry stays at her side until she is gone. He attempts to say goodbye but cannot. He walks back to his hotel in the rain.

CHARACTER LIST

Lieutenant Frederic Henry The novel's narrator and protagonist. A young American ambulance driver in the Italian army during World War I, Henry meets his military duties with quiet stoicism. He displays courage in battle, but his selfless motivations undermine all sense of glory and heroism, abstract terms for which Henry has little patience. His life lacks real passion until he meets the beautiful Catherine Barkley.

Catherine Barkley An English nurse's aide who falls in love with Henry. Catherine is exceptionally beautiful and possesses, perhaps, the most sensuously described hair in all of literature. When the novel opens, Catherine's grief for her dead fiancé launches her headlong into a playful, though reckless, game of seduction. Her feelings for Henry soon intensify and become more complicated, however, and she eventually swears lifelong fidelity to him.

Rinaldi A surgeon in the Italian army. Mischievous, wry, and oversexed, Rinaldi is Henry's closest friend. Although Rinaldi is a skilled doctor, his primary practice is seducing beautiful women. When Henry returns to Gorizia, Rinaldi tries to whip up a convivial atmosphere.

The priest A kind, sweet, young man who provides spiritual guidance to the few soldiers interested in it. Often the butt of the officers' jokes, the priest responds with good-natured understanding. Through Henry's conversations with him regarding the war, the novel challenges abstract ideals like glory, honor, and sacredness.

Helen Ferguson A nurse's aide who works at the American hospital and a dear friend of Catherine. Though Helen is friendly and accepting of Henry and Rinaldi's visits to Catherine early in the novel, her hysterical outburst over Henry and Catherine's "immoral" affair establishes her as an unhappy woman who is paranoid about her friend's safety and anxious about her own loneliness.

Miss Gage An American nurse who helps Henry through his recovery at the hospital in Milan. At ease and accepting, Miss Gage becomes a friend to Henry, someone with whom he can share a drink and gossip.

Miss Van Campen The superintendent of nurses at the American hospital in which Catherine works. Miss Van Campen is strict, cold, and unpleasant. She disapproves of Henry and remains on cool terms with him throughout his stay.

Dr. Valentini An Italian surgeon who comes to the American hospital to contradict the hospital's opinion that Henry must wait six months before having an operation on his leg. In agreeing to perform surgery the next morning, Dr. Valentini displays the kind of self-assurance and confidence that Henry (and the novel) celebrates.

Count Greffi A spry, ninety-four-year-old nobleman. The count represents a more mature version of Henry's character and Hemingway's masculine ideal. He lives life to the fullest and thinks for himself. Though the count dismisses the label "wise," Henry clearly values his thoughts and sees him as a sort of father figure.

Ettore Moretti An American soldier from San Francisco. Ettore, like Henry, fights for the Italian army. Unlike Henry, however, Ettore is an obnoxious braggart. Quick to instigate a fight or display the medals that he claims to have worked so hard to win, he believes in and pursues the glory and honor that Henry eschews.

Gino   A young Italian whom Henry meets at a decimated village. Gino's patriotic belief that his fatherland is sacred and should be protected at all costs contrasts sharply to Henry's attitude toward war.

Ralph Simmons An opera student of dubious talent. Simmons is the first person that Henry goes to see after fleeing from battle. Simmons proves to be a generous friend, giving Henry civilian clothes so that he can travel to Switzerland without drawing suspicion.

Emilio   A bartender in the town of Stresa. Emilio proves a good friend to Henry and Catherine, helping them reunite, saving them from arrest, and ushering them off to safety.

Bonello   An ambulance driver under Henry's command. Bonello displays his ruthlessness when he brutally unloads a pistol round into the head of an uncooperative engineer whom Henry has already shot.

Analysis of Major Characters

Frederic Henry

In the sections of the novel in which he describes his experience in the war, Henry portrays himself as a man of duty. He attaches to this understanding of himself no sense of honor, nor does he expect any praise for his service. Even after he has been severely wounded, he discourages Rinaldi from pursuing medals of distinction for him. Time and again, through conversations with men like the priest, Ettore Moretti, and Gino, Henry distances himself from such abstract notions as faith, honor, and patriotism. Concepts such as these mean nothing to him beside such concrete facts of war as the names of the cities in which he has fought and the numbers of decimated streets.

Against this bleak backdrop, Henry's reaction to Catherine Barkley is rather astonishing. The reader understands why Henry responds to the game that Catherine proposes—why he pledges his love to a woman he barely knows: like Rinaldi, he hopes for a night's simple pleasures. But an active sex drive does not explain why Henry returns to Catherine—why he continues to swear his love even after Catherine insists that he stop playing. In his fondness for Catherine, Henry reveals a vulnerability usually hidden by his stoicism and masculinity. The quality of the language that Henry uses to describe Catherine's hair and her presence in bed testifies to the genuine depth of his feelings for her. Furthermore, because he allows Henry to narrate the book, Hemingway is able to suffuse the entire novel with the power and pathos of an elegy: *A Farewell to Arms,* which Henry narrates after Catherine's death, confirms his love and his loss.

Catherine Barkley

Much has been written regarding Hemingway's portrayal of female characters. With the advent of feminist criticism, readers have become more vocal about their dissatisfaction with Hemingway's depictions of women, which, according to critics such as Leslie A. Fiedler, tend to fall into one of two categories: overly dominant shrews, like Lady Brett in *The Sun Also Rises,* and overly submissive confections, like Catherine Barkley in *A Farewell to Arms.* Hemingway, Fiedler maintains, was at his best dealing with men without women; when he started to involve female characters in his writing, he reverted to uncomplicated stereotypes. *A Farewell to Arms* certainly supports such a reading: it is easy to see how Catherine's blissful submission to domesticity, especially at the novel's end, might rankle contemporary readers for whom lines such as "I'm having a child and that makes me contented not to do anything" suggest a bygone era in which a woman's work centered around maintaining a home and filling it with children.

Still, even though Catherine's excessive desire to live a lovely life may, at times, make her more archetypal than real, it is unfair to deny her the nuances of her character. Although Catherine alludes to her initial days with Henry as a period when she was slightly "crazy," she seems perfectly aware of the fact that she and Henry are, at first, playing an elaborate game of seduction. Rather than being swept off her feet by Henry's declarations of love, she capably draws the line, telling him when she has had enough for the night or reminding him that their budding love is a lie. In fact, Catherine's resistance holds out much longer than Henry's: even after Henry emphatically states that he loves her and that their lives together will be splendid, Catherine exhibits the occasional doubt, telling him that she is sure that dreadful things await them and claiming that she fears having a baby because she has never loved anyone. Privy only to what Catherine says, not to what she thinks, the reader is left to explain these infrequent lapses in her otherwise uncompromised devotion. Her premonition of dreadful things, for instance, may simply be a general alarm about the war-torn world or residual guilt for loving a man other than the fiancé whom she is mourning as the book opens. While the degree to which Catherine is conflicted remains open to debate, her loyalty to Henry does not. She is a loving, dedicated woman whose desire and capacity for a redemptive, otherworldly love makes her the inevitable victim of tragedy.

RINALDI

Rinaldi's character serves an important function in *A Farewell to Arms*. He dominates an array of minor male characters who embody the kind of virile, competent, and good-natured masculinity that, for better or worse, so much of Hemingway's fiction celebrates. Rinaldi is an unbelievable womanizer, professing to be in love with Catherine at the beginning of the novel but claiming soon thereafter to be relieved that he is not, like Henry, saddled with the complicated emotional baggage that the love of a woman entails. Considering Rinaldi's frequent visits to the local whorehouses, Henry later muses that his friend has most likely succumbed to syphilis. While this registers as an unpleasant end, it is presented with an air of detached likelihood rather than fervent moralizing. It is, in other words, not punishment for a man's bad behavior but rather the consequence of a man behaving as a man—living large, living boldly, and being true to himself.

THEMES, MOTIFS & SYMBOLS

THEMES

Themes are the fundamental and often universal ideas explored in a literary work.

THE GRIM REALITY OF WAR

As the title of the novel makes clear, *A Farewell to Arms* concerns itself primarily with war, namely the process by which Frederic Henry removes himself from it and leaves it behind. The few characters in the novel who actually support the effort—Ettore Moretti and Gino—come across as a dull braggart and a naïve youth, respectively. The majority of the characters remain ambivalent about the war, resentful of the terrible destruction it causes, doubtful of the glory it supposedly brings.

The novel offers masterful descriptions of the conflict's senseless brutality and violent chaos: the scene of the Italian army's retreat remains one of the most profound evocations of war in American literature. As the neat columns of men begin to crumble, so too do the soldiers' nerves, minds, and capacity for rational thought and moral judgment. Henry's shooting of the engineer for refusing to help free the car from the mud shocks the reader for two reasons: first, the violent outburst seems at odds with Henry's coolly detached character; second, the incident occurs in a setting that robs it of its moral import—the complicity of Henry's fellow soldiers legitimizes the killing. The murder of the engineer seems justifiable because it is an inevitable by-product of the spiraling violence and disorder of the war.

Nevertheless, the novel cannot be said to condemn the war; *A Farewell to Arms* is hardly the work of a pacifist. Instead, just as the innocent engineer's death is an inevitability of war, so is war the inevitable outcome of a cruel, senseless world. Hemingway suggests that war is nothing more than the dark, murderous extension of a world that refuses to acknowledge, protect, or preserve true love.

THE RELATIONSHIP BETWEEN LOVE AND PAIN

Against the backdrop of war, Hemingway offers a deep, mournful meditation on the nature of love. No sooner does Catherine announce to Henry that she is in mourning for her dead fiancé than she begins a game meant to seduce Henry. Her reasons for doing so are clear: she wants to distance herself from the pain of her loss. Likewise, Henry intends to get as far away from talk of the war as possible. In each other, Henry and Catherine find temporary solace from the things that plague them. The couple's feelings for each other quickly pass from an amusement that distracts them to the very fuel that sustains them. Henry's understanding of how meaningful his love for Catherine is outweighs any consideration for the emptiness of abstract ideals such as honor, enabling him to flee the war and seek her out. Reunited, they plan an idyllic life together that promises to act as a salve for the damage that the war has inflicted. Far away from the decimated Italian countryside, each intends to be the other's refuge. If they are to achieve physical, emotional, and psychological healing, they have found the perfect place in the safe remove of the Swiss mountains. The tragedy of the novel rests in the fact that their love, even when genuine, can never be more than temporary in this world.

MOTIFS

Motifs are recurring structures, contrasts, and literary devices that can help to develop and inform the text's major themes.

MASCULINITY

Readers of Hemingway's fiction will quickly notice a consistent thread in the portrayal and celebration of a certain kind of man: domineering, supremely competent, and swaggeringly virile. *A Farewell to Arms* holds up several of its minor male characters as examples of fine manhood. Rinaldi is a faithful friend and an oversexed womanizer; Dr. Valentini exhibits a virility to rival Rinaldi's as well as a bold competence that makes him the best surgeon. Similarly, during the scene in which Henry fires his pistol at the fleeing engineering sergeants, Bonello takes charge of the situation by brutally shooting the fallen engineer in the head. The respect with which Hemingway sketches these men, even at their lowest points, is highlighted by the humor, if not contempt, with which he depicts their opposites. The success of each of these men depends, in part, on the failure of another: Rinaldi secures his sexual prowess by attacking the priest's lack of lust; Dr. Valentini's reputation as a surgeon is thrown into relief by the three mousy, overly cautious, and physically unimpressive doctors who precede him; and Bonello's ruthlessness is prompted by the disloyal behavior of the soldier whom he kills.

GAMES AND DIVERTISSEMENT

Henry and Catherine begin flirting with each other in order to forget personal troubles. Flirting, which Henry compares to bridge, allows Henry to "drop the war" and diverts Catherine's thoughts from the death of her fiancé. Likewise, the horse races that Catherine and Henry attend enable them to block out thinking of Henry's return to the front and of their imminent separation. Ironically, Henry and Catherine's relationship becomes the source of suffering from which Henry needs diversion. Henry cannot stand to be away from Catherine, and while playing pool with Count Greffi takes his mind off of her, the best divertissement turns out to be the war itself. When Catherine instructs him not to think about her when they are apart, Henry replies, "That's how I worked it at the front. But there was something to do then." The transformations of the war from fatal threat into divertissement and love from distraction into pain signal not only Henry's attachment to Catherine but also the transitory nature of happiness. Pathos radiates from this fleeting happiness because, even though happiness is temporary, the pursuit of it remains necessary. Perhaps an understanding of the limits of happiness explains the count's comment that though he values love most in life, he is not wise for doing so. The count is wiser than he claims, however. He hedges against the transitory nature of love by finding pleasure and amusement in games, birthday parties, and the taking of "a little stimulant." That one can depend on their simple pleasures lends games and divertissement a certain dignity; while they may not match up to the nobility of pursuits such as love, they prove quietly constant.

LOYALTY VERSUS ABANDONMENT

The notions of loyalty and abandonment apply equally well to love and war. The novel, however, suggests that loyalty is more a requirement of love and friendship than of the grand political causes and abstract philosophies of battling nations. While Henry takes seriously his duty as a lieutenant, he does not subscribe to the ideals that one typically imagines fuel soldiers in combat. Unlike Ettore Moretti or Gino, the promise of honor and the duties of patriotism

MOTIFS

mean little to Henry. Although he shoots an uncooperative engineering sergeant for failing to comply with his orders, Henry's violence should be read as an inevitable outcome of a destructive war rather than as a conscious decision to enforce a code of moral conduct. Indeed, Henry eventually follows in the engineering sergeants' footsteps by abandoning the army and his responsibilities. While he does, at times, feel guilt over this course of action, he takes comfort in the knowledge that he is most loyal where loyalty counts most: in his relationship with Catherine. That these conflicting allegiances cannot be reconciled does not suggest, however, that loyalty and abandonment lie at opposite ends of a moral spectrum. Rather, they reflect the priorities of a specific individual's life.

ILLUSIONS AND FANTASIES

Upon meeting, Catherine and Henry rely upon a grand illusion of love and seduction for comfort. Catherine seeks solace for the death of her fiancé, while Henry will do anything to distance himself from the war. At first, their declarations of love are transparent: Catherine reminds Henry several times that their courtship is a game, sending him away when she has played her fill. After Henry is wounded, however, his desire for Catherine and the comfort and support that she offers becomes more than a distraction from the world's unpleasantness; his love begins to sustain him and blossoms into something undeniably real. Catherine's feelings for Henry follow a similar course.

While the couple acts in ways that confirm the genuine nature of their passion, however, they never escape the temptation of dreaming of a better world. In other words, the boundary between reality and illusion proves difficult to identify. After Henry and Catherine have spent months of isolation in Switzerland, Hemingway depicts their relationship as a mixture of reality and illusion. Boredom has begun to set in, and the couple effects small daily changes to reinvigorate their lives and their passion: Catherine gets a new haircut, while Henry grows a beard. Still, or perhaps because of, the comparative dullness of real life (not to mention the ongoing war), the couple turns to fantasies of a more perfect existence. They dream of life on a Swiss mountain, where they will make their own clothes and need nothing but each other, suggesting that fantasizing is part of coping with the banal, sometimes damaging effects of reality.

SYMBOLS

Symbols are objects, characters, figures, and colors used to represent abstract ideas or concepts.

RAIN

Rain serves in the novel as a potent symbol of the inevitable disintegration of happiness in life. Catherine infuses the weather with meaning as she and Henry lie in bed listening to the storm outside. As the rain falls on the roof, Catherine admits that the rain scares her and says that it has a tendency to ruin things for lovers. Of course, no meteorological phenomenon has such power; symbolically, however, Catherine's fear proves to be prophetic, for doom does eventually come to the lovers. After Catherine's death, Henry leaves the hospital and walks home in the rain. Here, the falling rain validates Catherine's anxiety and confirms one of the novel's main contentions: great love, like anything else in the world—good or bad, innocent or deserving—cannot last.

CATHERINE'S HAIR

Although it is not a recurring symbol, Catherine's hair is an important one. In the early, easy days of their relationship, as Henry and Catherine lie in bed, Catherine takes down her hair and lets it cascade around Henry's head. The tumble of hair reminds Henry of being enclosed inside a tent or behind a waterfall. This lovely description stands as a symbol of the couple's isolation from the world. With a war raging around them, they manage to secure a blissful seclusion, believing themselves protected by something as delicate as hair. Later, however, when they are truly isolated from the ravages of war and living in peaceful Switzerland, they learn the harsh lesson that love, in the face of life's cruel reality, is as fragile and ephemeral as hair.

Summary & Analysis

Chapters I–V

Summary: Chapter I

The narrator, Lieutenant Henry, describes the small Italian village in which he lives. It is a summer during World War I, and troops often march along the road toward the nearby battlefront. Officers speed by in "small gray motor cars." If one of these cars travels especially fast, Henry speculates, it is probably carrying the king, who makes trips out to assess the battle almost every day. At the start of the winter, a cholera epidemic sweeps through the army and kills seven thousand soldiers.

Summary: Chapter II

Lieutenant Henry's unit moves to the town of Gorizia, further from the fighting, which continues in the mountains beyond. Life in Gorizia is relatively enjoyable: the buildings are not badly damaged, and there are nice cafés and two brothels—one for officers, one for enlisted men. One winter day, Henry sits in the mess hall with a group of fellow officers, who declare that the war is over for the year because of the snow. Spurred by their contempt for religion, the men taunt the military priest, baiting him with crude innuendos about his sexuality. A captain jokingly chides the priest for never cavorting with women, and the good-natured priest blushes. Though he is not religious, Henry treats the priest kindly. The officers then argue over where Henry should take his leave. The priest suggests that he visit the Abruzzi region, where the priest's family resides, but the officers have other ideas. They encourage him to visit Palermo, Capri, Rome, Naples, or Sicily. Soon the conversation turns to opera singers, and the officers retire to the whorehouse.

Summary: Chapter III

When he returns from his leave, Henry discusses his trip with his roommate, the lieutenant and surgeon Rinaldi. Henry claims to have traveled throughout Italy, and Rinaldi, who is obsessed with "beautiful girls," tells him that travel is no longer necessary to find such women. He reports that beautiful English women have been sent to the front and that he has fallen in love with a nurse named

Catherine Barkley. Henry loans him fifty lire (the plural of "lira," the Italian unit of currency) so that Rinaldi can give the woman the impression of being a wealthy man. At dinner that night, the priest is hurt that Henry failed to visit Abruzzi. Henry, feeling guilty, drunkenly explains that he wanted to make the visit but circumstances prevented him from doing so. By the end of the meal, the officers resume picking on the priest.

SUMMARY: CHAPTER IV
The next morning, a battery of guns wakes Henry. He goes to the garage, where the mechanics are working on a number of ambulances. He chats briefly with the men and then returns to his room, where Rinaldi convinces him to tag along on a visit to Miss Barkley. At the British Hospital, Rinaldi spends his time talking with Helen Ferguson, another nurse, while Henry becomes acquainted with Catherine. Henry is immediately struck by her beauty, especially her long blonde hair. She carries a stick that resembles a "toy riding-crop"; when Henry asks what it is, she confides that it belonged to her fiancé, who was killed in the Battle of the Somme. When she, in turn, asks if he has ever loved, Henry says no. On the way home, Rinaldi observes that Catherine prefers Henry to him.

SUMMARY: CHAPTER V
The next day, Henry calls on Catherine again. The head nurse expresses surprise that an American would want to join the Italian army. She tells him that Miss Barkley is on duty and unavailable to visitors until her shift ends at seven o'clock that evening. Henry drives back along the trenches, investigating the road that, when completed, will allow for an offensive attack. After dinner, Henry returns to see Catherine. He finds her in the garden with Helen Ferguson; Helen soon excuses herself. After chatting about Catherine's job, Henry and Catherine agree to "drop the war" as a subject of conversation. Henry tries to put his arm around her. She resists but, in the end, lets him. When he moves to kiss her, however, she slaps him. Their little drama, Henry notes with amusement, has gotten them away from talk of the war. Catherine lets Henry kiss her and begins to cry, saying, "We're going to have a strange life." Henry returns home, where Rinaldi teases him about his romantic glow.

ANALYSIS: CHAPTERS 1–5
Many critics maintain that Ernest Hemingway did more to change the tenor of twentieth-century American fiction than any other

writer. He favored a boldly declarative, pared-down prose style, which readers of the 1920s and 1930s considered a wildly experimental departure from the baroque, Victorian-influenced style that was then the standard for high literature. The short first chapter, in which Frederic Henry describes his situation on the war front, is one of the most famous descriptive passages in American literature. Hemingway sketches the description with a detached, almost journalistic prose style that is nevertheless emotionally poignant: "The trunks of the trees too were dusty and the leaves fell early that year and we saw the troops marching along the road and the dust rising and leaves. . . ." With relatively few but remarkably precise details, Hemingway captures life on the battlefront of a small Italian town during World War I.

In his *Death in the Afternoon,* a meditation on the arts of bullfighting and writing, Hemingway advocates an "Iceberg Theory" of fiction:

> *If a writer of prose knows enough about what he is writing about he may omit things that he knows and the reader, if the writer is writing truly enough, will have a feeling of those things as strongly as though the writer had stated them. The dignity of movement of an iceberg is due to only one-eighth of it being above water.*

True to Hemingway's ideal, the above description of trees, leaves, and a dusty road leaves the reader with more than a simple sense of Henry's environment. The lieutenant's language, mournful and repetitive as an elegy, hints at the great losses that he will eventually suffer.

Once Henry picks up the narrative in Gorizia, the reader is introduced to several of the novel's major characters and themes. Rinaldi immediately emerges as a vibrant and mischievous character (only Henry's word positions him as a passionate and committed surgeon). Henry soon establishes himself as a conflicted soldier. Having joined the army with neither a thirst for glory nor a fierce belief in its cause, Henry is physically, psychologically, and morally drained by the war. He is not alone. Catherine Barkley, who is tense and unnerving the first time Henry meets her, softens toward him quickly. Her strange behavior—the haste with which she attaches herself to a man whom she barely knows—belies the grief that she feels over the death of her fiancé.

Two dominant themes in *A Farewell to Arms* are love and war. War, which is described with brutal intensity, fills the mind of everyone in Henry's world. Thoughts of it afflict the characters like a painful, chronic headache. War fuels the sense of despair and grief at the heart of the book, establishing the harsh conditions whereby the loss of seven thousand soldiers to a cholera epidemic can be considered nominal. As Henry's initial conversations with Catherine make clear, everyone is desperate for an antidote to the numbing effects of war. People would prefer to think any other thoughts, to feel any other emotions, and so plunge headlong into love as a means of overcoming their fear, pain, and grief. Rinaldi pretends to love every beautiful woman he meets, while Catherine and Henry, upon meeting, play a seductively distracting game in which they pretend to love and care for each other.

CHAPTERS VI–IX

SUMMARY: CHAPTER VI

After spending two days at "the posts," Henry visits Catherine again. She asks him if he loves her and he says yes. She tells him to call her by her first name. They walk through the garden, and Catherine expresses how much she loves him and says how awful the past few days have been without him. Henry kisses her, thinking that she is "probably a little crazy," but not caring. Aware that he does not love Catherine, Henry feels that he is involved in a complicated game, like bridge. To his surprise, she acknowledges their charade, asking, "This is a rotten game we play, isn't it?" She assures him that she's not crazy, and, though they are no longer playing, he persuades her to kiss him. She breaks from the kiss suddenly and sends him away for the night. At home, Rinaldi senses Henry's romantic confusion and admits to feeling relieved that he himself did not become involved with a British nurse.

SUMMARY: CHAPTER VII

Driving back from his post the next afternoon, Henry picks up a soldier with a hernia. The man admits that he threw away his truss (a support for a hernia) on purpose so that he would not have to return to the front. He fears being turned over to his commanding officers, aware that they are familiar with this trick. Henry instructs the man to give himself a bump on the head, which he does, thereby earning his way into the hospital. Henry thinks about the upcoming offensive, which is scheduled to start in two days. He wishes that he were with Catherine, enjoying a hot night and good wine in Milan. At dinner, the men drink and tease the priest. Rinaldi escorts the drunken Henry to the British hospital, feeding him coffee beans to sober him up. At the nurses' villa, Helen Ferguson tells Henry that Catherine is sick and will not see him. Henry feels surprisingly "lonely and hollow."

SUMMARY: CHAPTER VIII
The next day, Henry hears of an attack scheduled for that night. As the cars pass the British hospital on their way to the front, Henry tells the driver of his car to stop. He hurries in and asks to see Catherine. He tells her that he is off for "a show" and that she shouldn't be worried. She gives him a St. Anthony medal to protect him. Henry returns to the car and the caravan continues toward Pavla, where the fighting will take place.

CHAPTER IX
At Pavla, Henry sees roadside trenches filled with artillery and Austrian observation balloons hanging ominously above the distant hills. A major greets Henry and his drivers and installs them in a dugout. The men talk disparagingly about the various ranks of soldiers and engage Henry in a discussion about ending the war. Henry maintains that they would all be worse off if the Italian army decided to stop fighting, but Passini, one of the ambulance drivers, respectfully disagrees, maintaining that the war will go on forever unless one side decides to stop. The men are hungry, so Henry and Gordini, another driver, fetch some cold macaroni and a slab of cheese from the main wound-dressing station. As they return to the dugout, shelling begins and bombs burst around them. As the men eat the food, there is "a flash, as when a blast-furnace door is swung open." Henry finds himself unable to breathe and thinks himself about to die. A trench mortar has exploded through the dugout, killing Passini and injuring Gordini. The two remaining drivers, Gavuzzi and Manera, carry Henry to a wound-dressing station, where a British doctor treats Henry's ruined leg. An ambulance is loaded with the wounded and sent off to the hospital.

ANALYSIS: CHAPTERS VI–IX
Henry's small personal stake in the war, toward which he displays a supreme indifference, becomes increasingly clear in these chapters. As an American soldier fighting in the Italian army—an army that Catherine and the other British nurses don't take seriously—Henry feels as detached from the war as he feels from everything else in his life. He claims that the war does "not have anything to do with me,"

and he feels no real commitment to it. His behavior with the soldier who admits to tossing away his truss in order to worsen his hernia and thereby evade service is telling; Henry exhibits none of the integrity that the reader might expect of the young man's commanding officer. Rather than chastise him for his self-serving, irresponsible attitude, Henry helps him plot his way into the hospital, thereby contributing, in a small way, to the overall deterioration of the Italian army.

Henry's behavior with the ambulance drivers further establishes his detachment from the war. The men feel comfortable voicing their contempt for the soldiers and their belief that Italy should withdraw from the war in front of Henry, though they know better than to "talk so other officers can hear." Although Henry defends the Italian army and the war effort, he does so from a calm, philosophical standpoint rather than anger at the men's disrespect. Also noteworthy is that Henry risks his life for something as inglorious as a slab of cheese. The scene in which he braves falling mortar shells in order to dress his pasta upends the popular literary convention of the protagonist facing great adversity to accomplish a noble end. Henry's objective is ridiculous, pathetic, and decidedly not heroic. That this scene follows on the heels of a conversation in which the men maintain that "war is not won by victory" amplifies the doubt cast upon romantic ideals such as glory and honor.

At this point in the novel, and especially in his dealings with the ambulance drivers, Henry comes off as rather stoic. His engagement with the men as they discuss victory and defeat seems academic rather than passionate; he appears indifferent to the sense of loss, fear, and anger that fuels the Italians' arguments, indifferent even to whether he lives or dies. In this context, his recurring thoughts of, and increasing feeling for, Catherine are somewhat curious. The notion of visiting her interrupts his daydreaming about the war the night before he leaves for the front. In a very beautiful, sensuous passage, Henry imagines himself and Catherine stealing away to a hotel, where she pretends that he is her dead lover: "we would drink the capri and the door locked and it hot and only a sheet and the whole night and we would both love each other all night in the hot night in Milan." Even though his attachment to Catherine is, at this point, casual, Henry is beginning to develop feelings that extend beyond the game he plays with her. The sorrow that he feels when Helen Ferguson announces that Catherine is sick and cannot see him surprises him and hints at the depth of feeling, commitment, and attachment of which this usually stoic soldier is capable.

Chapters X–XIII

Summary: Chapter X

At the field hospital, Henry lies in intense pain. Rinaldi comes to visit and informs Henry that he, Henry, will be decorated for heroism in battle. Henry protests, declaring that he displayed no heroism, but Rinaldi insists. He leaves Henry with a bottle of cognac and promises to send Catherine to see him soon.

Summary: Chapter XI

At dusk, the priest comes to visit. He tells Henry that he misses him at the mess hall and offers gifts of mosquito netting, a bottle of vermouth, and English newspapers, for which Henry is grateful. The men drink and discuss the war. Henry admits to hating it, and the priest theorizes that there are two types of men in the world: those who would make war and those who would not. Henry laments that "the first ones make [the second ones] do it . . . And I help them." Henry wonders if ending the war is a hopeless effort; the priest assures him that it is not, but admits that he, too, has trouble hoping. The conversation turns to God, and the priest defends his beliefs against the other officers' teasing. A man who loves God, he says, is not a dirty joke. Henry cannot say that he loves God, but he does admit to fearing Him sometimes. The priest concludes by telling Henry that he, Henry, has a capacity to love. He makes a distinction between sleeping with women at brothels and giving fully of oneself to another human being, and assures Henry that, eventually, he will be called upon to love truly. Henry remains skeptical. The priest says goodbye, and Henry falls asleep.

Summary: Chapter XII

The doctors are anxious to ship Henry to Milan, where he can receive better treatment for his injured knee and leg. They are eager to get the wounded soldiers fixed up or transferred as quickly as possible because all of the hospital beds will be needed when the offensive begins. The night before Henry leaves for Milan, Rinaldi and a major from Henry's company return for a visit. America has just declared war on Germany, and the Italians are very excited and hopeful. Rinaldi asks if President Wilson will declare war on Austria, and Henry responds that Wilson will within days. The men get drunk, discussing the war and life in Milan. Rinaldi reports that Catherine will be going to serve at the hospital in Milan. The following morning, Henry sets off for Milan. He describes the train ride, during which he gets so drunk that he vomits on the floor.

SUMMARY: CHAPTER XIII

Two days later, Henry arrives in Milan and is taken to the American hospital. Two ambulance drivers carry him inside clumsily, causing him a great amount of pain. In the ward, the men are met by an easily frazzled, gray-haired nurse named Mrs. Walker, who cannot get Henry a room without a doctor's orders. Henry asks the men to carry him into a room and goes to sleep. The next morning, a young nurse named Miss Gage arrives to take his temperature. Mrs. Walker returns and, together with Miss Gage, changes Henry's bed. In the afternoon, the superintendent of the hospital, Miss Van Campen, appears and introduces herself. She and Henry take an immediate dislike to each other. Henry asks for wine with his meals, but Miss Van Campen says that wine is out of the question unless prescribed by a doctor. Later, Henry sends for a porter to bring him several bottles of wine and the evening papers. Before Henry goes to sleep, Miss Van Campen sends him something of a peace offering: a glass of eggnog spiked with sherry.

ANALYSIS: CHAPTERS X–XIII

Henry's unemotional reaction to being wounded further displays his stoicism: he exhibits neither despair at the wound itself nor excitement at Rinaldi's promise that the wound will bring him glory. As his conversation with Rinaldi makes clear, he has no interest in being decorated with medals. Despite Henry's aloofness, however, his chat with Rinaldi furthers a sympathetic impression of how men behave toward, and care for, one another. While allegiance to their countries is, in a way, voluntary—after all, no one *wants* to fight this war—men are expected to show unconditional loyalty to their friends. This expectation adds to a code of conduct partially expounded upon earlier when the officers harass the priest for his lack of sexual exploits. Loyalty, strength, resilience in the face of adversity, and a healthy sexual appetite—these are the traditional tropes of masculinity that the novel celebrates.

In light of Henry's indifference to war medals, it is interesting to note the arguable connection between Hemingway's Henry and another Henry—Stephen Crane's Henry Fleming, the initially overzealous and glory-seeking protagonist of *The Red Badge of Courage*. Toward the end of Crane's Civil War masterpiece, which

Hemingway greatly admired and included in his 1942 collection *Men at War: The Best War Stories of All Time,* Fleming's self-absorption dissolves into a mature and quiet dignity. One can make a strong case that the stoic Frederic Henry is an outgrowth of this newly self-possessed and respectable Henry Fleming.

Rinaldi, with his endless talk about "pretty girls" and frequent trips to the brothel, embodies the overactive male sex drive. But, as the priest suggests in his conversation with Henry, sex is not enough to satisfy a man. The priest believes that Henry lacks someone to love and, when Henry protests, draws a distinction between lust for prostitutes, of which there is no shortage among the soldiers, and true, profound love. Love, in the priest's estimation, makes a man want to give of himself, to make sacrifices for the sake of another. Although Henry remains unconvinced, his increasing affection for Catherine hints that he will inevitably experience the kind of passionate and meaningful connection that the priest describes.

The characters in *A Farewell to Arms* are constantly seeking solace from a world ravaged by war. This solace, most often and most simply, comes in the form of alcohol. Throughout the novel, vast amounts of wine and liquor are consumed. Henry depends upon alcohol, and goes so far as to consider it a necessary part of his convalescence: when Miss Van Campen refuses him wine with his meals, he immediately arranges to have some smuggled into the hospital. This sort of escape is understandable, given the reader's growing impression of the folly of war. Just as Henry is scornful of medals and the honor that they supposedly bestow, the novel questions whether war is truly an appropriate forum for such lofty and romantic distinctions. As evidenced by the preposterous purpose for which Henry risks his life in battle—getting some cheese to top his pasta—the novel severs any traditional association between battle and glory. Similarly, once Henry arrives at the hospital in Milan, the reader witnesses an equally pathetic and ludicrous world in which clumsy ambulance drivers cannot manage the weight of a wounded soldier and inept nurses cry rather than care for their patients.

CHAPTERS XIV–XVII

SUMMARY: CHAPTER XIV

In the morning, Miss Gage shows Henry the vermouth bottle that she found under his bed. He fears that she will get him into trouble, but, instead, she wonders why he did not ask her to join him for a drink. She reports that Miss Barkley has come to work at the hospital and that she does not like her. Henry assures her that she will. At Henry's request, a barber arrives to shave him. The man treats Henry very rudely, and the porter later explains that he had mistaken Henry for an Austrian soldier and was close to cutting his throat. The misunderstanding causes the porter much amusement. After the barber and the porter leave, Catherine enters, and Henry realizes that he is in love with her. He pulls her onto the bed with him, and they make love for the first time.

SUMMARY: CHAPTER XV

Henry meets a thin, little doctor who removes some of the shrapnel from his leg, but whose "fragile delicacy" is soon exhausted by the task. The doctor sends Henry for an X-ray. Later, three doctors arrive to consult on the case. They agree that Henry should wait six months before having an operation. Henry jokes that he would rather have them amputate the leg. As he cannot stand the thought of spending so long in bed, he asks for another opinion. Two hours later, Dr. Valentini arrives. Valentini is cheerful, energetic, and competent. He has a drink with Henry and agrees to perform the necessary operation in the morning.

SUMMARY: CHAPTER XVI

> *"There, darling. Now you're all clean inside and out.*
> *Tell me. How many people have you ever loved?"*
> *"Nobody."*
>
> *(See* QUOTATIONS, *p. 49)*

Catherine spends the night in Henry's room. They lie in bed together, watching the night through the windows and a searchlight sweep across the ceiling. Henry worries that they will be discovered, but Catherine assures him that everyone is asleep and that they are safe. In the morning, Henry fancies going to the park to have breakfast, while Catherine prepares him for his operation. He urges her to come back to bed. She refuses and tells him that he probably will not want her later that night when he returns from surgery, groggy with an anesthetic. She warns him that such drugs tend to make patients chatty and begs him not to brag about their affair. They discuss their affair, and Catherine asks him how many women he has slept with. He answers none, and though she knows he is lying, she is pleased.

SUMMARY: CHAPTER XVII

After the operation, Henry grows very sick. As he recovers, three other patients come to the hospital—a boy from Georgia with malaria, a boy from New York with malaria and jaundice, and a boy who tried to unscrew the fuse cap from an explosive shell for a souvenir. Henry develops an appreciation for Helen Ferguson, who helps him pass notes to Catherine while she is on duty. He asks if she will come to their wedding, and Helen responds that she doubts that they will get married. Worried for her friend's health, Helen convinces Henry that Catherine should have a few nights off. Henry speaks frankly to Miss Gage about getting Catherine some time to rest. Catherine returns to Henry after three days, and they enjoy a passionate reunion.

ANALYSIS: CHAPTERS XIV–XVII

Just as the officers' early interactions with the priest establish the novel's sympathies toward a strong, virile type of male behavior, a number of peripheral characters who appear in Book Two (Chapters XIII–XXIV) strengthen this sentiment. Hemingway describes the doctor who begins to diagnose Henry's injuries as "a thin quiet little man who seemed disturbed by the war." While Henry himself is disturbed, if not sickened, by the war, he maintains a competence and self-assurance that set him apart from men like the doctor, who needs to consult a team of his colleagues. This doctor's character stands in sharp contrast to Dr. Valentini, a gregarious but competent surgeon who drinks hard and wears his sexual appetite on his sleeve. Valentini's presence contributes to the novel's celebration of a particular kind of manhood, a fraternal bond supported by a love of wine and women and by displays of reckless boldness, whether they happen on the battlefield, in the bedroom, or on the operating table.

Henry conforms to this type of masculine ideal by rushing boldly into a passionate affair with Catherine. When she appears in his room, he is struck by her beauty and declares the depth of his love for her in a single sentence: "Everything turned over inside of me." Henry's exchange with Catherine in Chapter XVI is incredibly powerful and suggestive. As they volley simple questions back and forth, asking whom the other has loved and made love to, the line between game-playing and true passion begins to blur. In between the lovers' terse, deceptively simple lines of dialogue, Hemingway manages to point the way toward reserves of untapped feeling. Both Henry and Catherine feel more than they say or can say. Grief, fear, and a profound desire to be protected from a hostile world are among the forces that bring them together. But these confessions are beyond them; rather, they speak in strikingly nonromantic terms:

> *"You've such a lovely temperature."*
> *"You've got a lovely everything."*
> *"Oh no. You have the lovely temperature. I'm awfully proud of your temperature."*

Such conversations might strike the reader as a silly, indulgent imitation of the way lovers speak to each other. Hemingway, however, rescues these lines from saccharine sentimentality by establishing a complex psychological motivation for them. For Henry and Catherine, such foolishly romantic lines offer a respite from their wartorn world. The frivolity and banality of their dialogue gauge their desire to escape the horror of the war.

Interestingly, in addition to being innovative, Hemingway's suggestive style of writing served a very practical purpose. The standards of decency in 1929 America would have barred a more explicit version of *A Farewell to Arms* from appearing in print. Hence, Hemingway hints at Henry and Catherine's first sexual encounter, demanding that his audience read between the lines. Even though such scenes spared puritanical readers explicit details, the novel was plagued by charges of indecency. A public outcry in Boston, for example, led to the excision of such perceived profanities as "balls" from the novel.

CHAPTERS XVIII–XXI

SUMMARY: CHAPTER XVIII

During the summer, Henry learns to walk on crutches, and he and Catherine enjoy their time together in Milan. They befriend the headwaiter at a restaurant called the Gran Italia, and Catherine continues to spend her nights with Henry. They pretend to themselves that they are married, though Henry admits that he is glad they are not. They discuss marriage: Catherine, sure that they would send a married woman away from the front, remains opposed to the idea. Marriage, she continues, is beside the point: "I couldn't be any more married." Catherine pledges to be faithful to Henry, saying that although she is sure "all sorts of dreadful things will happen to us," unfaithfulness is not one of them.

SUMMARY: CHAPTER XIX

When not with Catherine, Henry spends his time with various people from Milan. He keeps company with the Meyerses, an older couple who enjoy going to the races. One day, after running into the Meyerses on the street, Henry enters a shop and buys some chocolates for Catherine. At a nearby bar, he runs into Ettore Moretti, an Italian from San Francisco serving in the Italian army, and Ralph Simmons and Edgar Saunders, two opera singers. Ettore is very proud of his war medals and claims that he works hard for them. Henry calls the man a "legitimate hero" but notes that he is incredibly dull. When he reaches the hospital, he chats with Catherine, who cannot stand Moretti; she prefers the quieter, English gentleman-type heroes. As the couple talks on into the night, it begins to rain. Catherine fears the rain, which she claims is "very hard on loving," and begins to cry until Henry comforts her.

SUMMARY: CHAPTER XX

Henry and Catherine go to the races with Helen Ferguson, whom Henry calls "Fergie" or "Ferguson," and the boy who was wounded while trying to unscrew the nose cap on the shrapnel shell. They bet on horses based on Meyers's tips; Meyers usually bets successfully but shares his secrets very selectively. While watching the preparations for a race of horses that have never won a purse higher than 1,000 lire, Catherine spies a purplish-black horse that, she believes, has been dyed to disguise its true color. As Italian horse racing is rumored to be extremely corrupt, Catherine is sure that the horse is a champion in disguise. She and Henry bet their money on it but win much less than expected. Catherine eventually grows tired of the crowd, and she and Henry decide to watch the remaining races by themselves. They both claim to feel better, or less lonely, when they are alone together.

SUMMARY: CHAPTER XXI

By September, the Allied forces are suffering greatly. A British major reports to Henry that if things continue as they are, the Allies will be defeated in another year. He suggests, however, that such a development is fine so long as no one realizes it. As Henry's leg is nearly healed, he receives three weeks of convalescent leave, after which he will have to return to the front. Catherine offers to travel with him and then gives him a piece of startling news: she is three months pregnant. Catherine worries that Henry feels trapped and promises not to make trouble for him, but he tells her that he feels cheerful and that he thinks she is wonderful. Catherine talks about the obstacles they will face, and Henry states that a coward dies a thousand deaths, the brave but one. They wonder aloud who authored this observation, but neither is able to remember. Catherine then amends Henry's words, saying that intelligent brave men die perhaps two thousand deaths but never mention them.

ANALYSIS: CHAPTERS XVIII–XXI

This section of Book Two chronicles the happy summer that Henry and Catherine spend together before he must return to the front. As his leg heals, Henry enjoys increasing mobility, and he develops a more normal, social relationship with Catherine. One of the reasons that the reader is able to believe more fully in their relationship is that these chapters do much to develop Catherine's character. Whereas in earlier chapters Catherine can be read as an emotionally damaged woman who desperately craves companionship and protection, she now emerges as a more complicated and self-aware character. The trip to the racetrack, for example, shows her fundamental independence: she would rather lose money on a horse that she herself chooses than win based on a tip.

She exhibits this independence even further when she announces her pregnancy to Henry. Concerned that he will feel trapped or obligated, she offers to deal with the situation by herself. Whereas she earlier gushes determined, over-the-top romanticism, she now provides small reminders of the real and hostile world in which her relationship with Henry exists. Assuring him of her loyalty to him, she cannot help but admit, "I'm sure all sorts of dreadful things will happen to us." Even more striking is her admission, soon after announcing her pregnancy, that "I've never even loved anyone." We can access her intricate psychological state only partially. For instance, when she tells Henry, rather poetically, that she fears the rain because "it's very hard on loving," the reader can only begin to guess the kinds of sorrow, fear, and joy that have shaped her. As a result of our incomplete understanding of her, Catherine can appear somewhat underdeveloped as a character. But her loyalty to Henry and her courage remain strong and constant.

The introduction of Ettore Moretti brings Henry's character into greater focus by juxtaposing him with a sharp contrast. The Italian-American soldier is boastful, ambitious, and arrogant; he is quick to insult others, such as the tenor at whom, he claims, audiences throw benches, and equally quick to sing his own praises. Henry, on the other hand, is reserved, detached, and disciplined. Suspicious of, or simply uninterested in, the glory for which the army awards medals, Henry maintains a calm levelheadedness that helps to convince the reader that his feelings for Catherine are indeed genuine.

Henry's words about cowards echo Julius Caesar's defiant utterance in Shakespeare's play *Julius Caesar:* "Cowards die many times before their deaths; / The valiant never taste of death but once" (II. ii.32–33). Although Caesar's stoicism carries an arrogant refusal to believe that any harm can actually befall him, Henry, like Caesar, remains philosophical and unafraid in the face of potential peril. His inability to contextualize the reference suggests shortsightedness about the development of his relationship with Catherine. His failure to recognize that Caesar dies a few scenes after making this bold declaration seems to foreshadow disaster for Henry.

Chapters XXII–XXVI

Summary: Chapter XXII
The next morning, it begins to rain, and Henry is diagnosed with jaundice. Miss Van Campen finds empty liquor bottles in Henry's room and blames alcoholism for his condition. She accuses him of purposefully making himself ill in order to avoid being sent back to the front. She orders his liquor stash to be taken away and promises to file a report that will deny him his convalescent leave, which she successfully does.

Summary: Chapter XXIII
Henry prepares to travel back to the front. He says his goodbyes at the hospital and heads out to the streets. While passing a café, he sees Catherine in the window and knocks for her to join him. They pass a pair of lovers standing outside a cathedral. When Henry observes, "They're like us," Catherine unhappily responds, "Nobody is like us." They enter a gun shop, where Henry buys a new pistol and several ammunition cartridges. On the street, they kiss like the lovers outside the cathedral did. Henry suggests that they go somewhere private, and Catherine agrees. They find a hotel. Even though it is a nice hotel and Catherine stops on the way to buy an expensive nightgown, she still feels like a prostitute. After dinner, however, they both feel fine. Henry utters the lines, "'But at my back I always hear / Time's wingèd chariot hurrying near,'" which Catherine recognizes as a couplet from the poetry of Andrew Marvell. Henry asks Catherine how she will manage having the baby; she assures

him that she will be fine and that she will have set up a nice home for Henry by the time he returns.

SUMMARY: CHAPTER XXIV

Outside, Henry calls for a carriage to bring him and Catherine from the hotel to the train station. He gets out at the station and sends her on to the hospital. He begs her to take care of herself and "little Catherine." There is a small commotion on the crowded train because Henry has arranged for a machine-gunner to save him a seat. A tall, gaunt captain protests. Eventually, Henry offers the offended captain his seat and sleeps on the floor.

SUMMARY: CHAPTER XXV

After returning to Gorizia, Henry has a talk with the town major about the war. It was a bad summer, the major says. The major is pleased to learn that Henry received his decorations and decides that Henry was lucky to get wounded when he did. The major admits that he is tired of the war and states that he doesn't believe that he would come back if he were given leave from the front. Henry then goes to find Rinaldi, and while he waits for his friend, he thinks about Catherine. Rinaldi comes into the room and is glad to see Henry. He examines his friend's wounded knee and exclaims that it is a crime that Henry was sent back into battle. Rinaldi asks if Henry has married and if he is in love. He asks if Catherine is good in bed, which offends Henry, who says that he holds certain subjects "sacred." They drink a toast to Catherine and go down to dinner. Rinaldi halfheartedly picks on the priest, trying to animate the nearly deserted dining hall for Henry's sake.

SUMMARY: CHAPTER XXVI

After dinner, Henry talks with the priest. The priest thinks that the war will end soon, though he cannot say why he thinks so. Henry remains skeptical. The priest notices a change in the men, citing the major, whom he describes as "gentle," as an example. Henry speculates that defeat has made the men gentler and points the priest to the story of Jesus Christ, who, Henry suggests, was mild because he had been beaten down. Henry claims that he no longer believes in victory. At the end of the evening, when the priest asks what Henry *does* believe in, he responds, "In sleep."

ANALYSIS: CHAPTERS XXII–XXVI

If Catherine's behavior in the last section casts a slight shadow over the romantic idealism surrounding her relationship with Henry, her farewell to him casts it into darkness. A sense of doom slowly closes in. Catherine's observation, as she and Henry pass a young, amorous couple, that "nobody is like us" betrays the pathos at the heart of their relationship. By removing their relationship from the lofty realm of idealized love, Hemingway makes Catherine and Henry's love for each other more real, more complicated, and more convincing.

The lines of poetry that Henry quotes are from Andrew Marvell's poem "To His Coy Mistress" (1681). In the poem, a man addresses the young object of his desire and tries to convince her that the social norms that keep her chaste are unimportant in the face of inevitable death. Life is painfully short, the poem suggests; whatever pleasure can be had should be had regardless of fussy, moralistic traditions. The poem plays an important role in shaping the farewell scene between Catherine and Henry. In their hotel room, Catherine says that she feels like a whore; even though she feels no need to marry—and has asked Henry how they could possibly be more married than they are now—the strict moral expectations of society still exert a force strong enough to vex her happiness. She quickly overcomes this feeling and actually wants to do "something really sinful" with Henry. A sin, she imagines, would bring them closer together by throwing them into sharper contrast with the outside world. As she says at the racetrack, she feels she is at her best and least lonely when she and Henry are separated from everyone around them. The final lines of Marvell's poem evoke this aspect of Catherine and Henry's relationship:

> Let us roll all our strength, and all
> Our sweetness, up into one ball:
> And tear our pleasures with rough strife,
> Through the iron gates of life.

Given the lack of comforts in a world so ravaged by war, it is little wonder that Catherine wants to unite with Henry against life's harsh realities.

Henry's discussion with the priest confirms the difficulties of living in a world in which war has crumbled many of the foundations—God, love, honor—that help to structure human life and give it meaning. Those of Hemingway's characters who have not yet lost all sense of these beliefs, as Rinaldi has, try to make up for the loss in other ways, as Catherine does. Henry's conversation with the priest illustrates the numb horror one feels when there is nothing left in which to believe. Without a belief in God or a commitment to the war in which he is fighting, Henry can safely say that he believes only in the oblivion that sleep brings.

Chapters XXVII–XXIX

Summary: Chapter XXVII

> *Abstract words such as glory, honor, courage, or*
> *hallow were obscene beside the concrete . . . numbers*
> *of regiments and the dates.*
>
> (See QUOTATIONS, p. 50)

The next morning, Henry travels to the Bainsizza, a succession of small mountains in which intense fighting has taken place. Henry meets a man named Gino, who tells him about a battery of terrifying guns that the Austrians have. The men discuss the Italian army's position against Croatian troops; Gino predicts that there will be nowhere for the Italians to go should the Austrians decide to attack. He claims that the summer's losses were not in vain, and Henry falls silent, thinking how words like "sacred, glorious, and sacrifice" embarrass him. He believes that concrete facts, such as the names of villages and the numbers of streets, have more meaning than such abstractions.

That night, the rain comes down hard and the enemy begins a bombardment. In the morning, the Italians learn that the attacking forces include Germans, and they become very afraid. They have had little contact with the Germans in the war and would prefer to keep it that way. The next night, word arrives that the Italian line has been broken; the forces begin a large-scale retreat. The troops slowly move out. As they come to the town of Gorizia, Henry sees women from the soldiers' whorehouse being loaded into a truck. Bonello, one of the drivers under Henry's command, offers to go with the women. At the villa, Henry discovers that Rinaldi has taken off for the hospital; everyone else has evacuated too. Henry, Bonello, and two other drivers, Piani and Aymo, rest and eat before resuming the retreat.

SUMMARY: CHAPTER XXVIII

> *Then the truck stopped. The whole column was*
> *stopped. It started again and we went a little farther,*
> *then stopped.*
>
> (See QUOTATIONS, p. 51)

The men drive slowly through the town, forming an endless column of retreating soldiers and vehicles. Henry takes a turn sleeping; shortly after he wakes, the column stalls. Henry exits his vehicle to check on his men. He discovers two engineering officers in Bonello's car and two women with Aymo. The girls seem suspicious of Aymo's intentions, but he eventually, if crudely, convinces them that he means them no harm. Henry returns to Piani's car and falls asleep. His dreams are of Catherine, and he speaks aloud to her. That night, columns of peasants join the retreating army. In the early morning, Henry and his men decide to separate from the column and take a small road going north. They stop briefly at an abandoned farmhouse and eat a large breakfast before continuing their journey.

CHAPTER XXIX

Aymo's car gets stuck in the soft ground, and the men are forced to cut brush hurriedly to place under the tires for traction. Henry orders the two engineering sergeants riding with Bonello to help. Afraid of being overtaken by the enemy, they refuse and try to leave. Henry draws his gun and shoots one of them; the other escapes. Bonello takes Henry's pistol and finishes off the wounded soldier. The men use branches, twigs, and even clothing to create traction, but the car sinks further into the mud. They continue in the other vehicles but soon get stuck again. Henry gives some money to the two girls traveling with Aymo and sends them off to a nearby village. The men continue to Udine on foot.

ANALYSIS: CHAPTERS XXVII–XXIX

Hemingway's description of the retreat, which is based on one of the most large-scale retreats of World War I, is one of the most famous descriptive passages in the novel. As the lumbering columns of army vehicles wind through the country night, Hemingway's prose mimics the dark and streaming motion of the men. When the movement of the columns becomes choppy, so do Hemingway's sentences: "Then the truck stopped. The whole column was stopped. It started again and went a little farther, then stopped."

These three chapters are most noteworthy for their powerful, uncompromising, and unromantic evocation of war. As Henry reflects in his conversation with the priest, abstract concepts like courage and honor have no place alongside the concrete reality of war. In describing the retreat, Hemingway strips war of its romantic packaging and provides the reader with only the most solid, evocative, and precise details.

In Book Three (which begins with Chapter XXV), the focus of the novel switches noticeably from love, the major thematic interest of Book Two, to war. Hemingway reports from the battlefront with a neutral, journalistic style that heightens the realism of the narrative and proves surprisingly unsettling. When Henry shoots at the two engineering officers for refusing to help free the car from the mud, Hemingway's detached prose refrains from passing moral judgment on his action. Rather, the text offers just the facts. This spare, disinterested tone sets Henry's wanton violence against an amoral landscape; shooting a man out of anger is given the same weight as pushing a car out of the mud. Refusing to give the reader reliable moral ground from which he or she may view and judge the scene, Hemingway challenges the reader to deal with the scene on his or her own terms. Certainly, the support that Henry receives from his fellow soldiers suggests that his actions are not abnormal and that there is a larger, pervasive irrationality at work. Indeed, the lack of a well-defined sense of right and wrong in the narrative perspective mirrors the situation in which Henry finds himself. War has stripped the world of its certainties, leaving men to set their own moral compass. Some, like Gino, fight for their homeland because they believe in ideals such as sacred ground and sacrifice, while others, like Henry, attach no such grandeur or meaning to their behavior on the battlefield.

The murder of the engineering officer is a testament to Hemingway's brilliant depiction of the confusion and meaninglessness of war. This act seemingly comes out of nowhere. The reader doesn't expect the normally self-possessed Henry to display such aggression, nor does such behavior seem particularly justified. Bonello's ruthless, point-blank extermination of the man's life is equally senseless. That the engineer is guilty of no capital crime and thus merits no punishment so grave as death emphasizes that, oftentimes, one cannot account for men's behavior in war.

Chapters XXX–XXXII

Summary: Chapter XXX

Crossing a bridge, Henry sees a German staff car crossing another bridge nearby. Aymo soon spots a heavily armed bicycle troop. Fearing capture, Henry and the men decide to avoid the main road, which the retreat follows, and head for the smaller secondary roads. They start down an embankment and are shot at. A bullet hits Aymo and kills him almost instantly. Realizing that their friend has been shot by their own troops—the Italian rear guard, which is afraid of everything—Henry and his men realize that they are in more danger than they would be facing the enemy. They look for a place to hide until dark and come across an abandoned farmhouse.

Henry camps out in the hayloft, while Piani and Bonello search for food. Piani returns alone and reports that Bonello, fearing death, left the farm in hopes of being taken prisoner and thereby escaping death. The men hide in the barn until nightfall and then set out to rejoin the Italians. They come upon a large gathering of soldiers where officers are being separated and interrogated for the "treachery" that led to an Italian defeat. Suddenly, two men from the battle police seize hold of Henry. He watches as a lieutenant colonel is led away, questioned, and shot to death. Sensing the opportunity to escape, Henry runs for the water and dives in. As he swims away he hears shots, but as he gains distance from shore, the sounds of gunfire fade.

Summary: Chapter XXXI

After floating in the cold river water for what seems to him a very long time, Henry climbs out, removes from his shirt the stars that identify him as an officer, and counts his money. He crosses the Venetian plain that day and jumps aboard a military train that evening. He freezes when a young soldier with a helmet that is too large for his head spots him, but the boy assumes that Henry belongs on the train and does nothing. Henry then hides in a car stocked with guns. While crawling under a huge canvas tarp, he cuts his head open. He waits for the blood to coagulate so that he can pick the dried blood off of his forehead. He does not want to be conspicuous when he gets out.

Summary: Chapter XXXII

Exhausted, lying under the canvas, Henry thinks about how well the knee upon which Dr. Valentini operated has held up under the circumstances. He reflects that his thoughts still belong to him, and thinks about Catherine, though he realizes that thinking about her without promise of seeing her might drive him crazy. Thoughts of loss plague him. Without his men, an army to which to return, or the friends that he remembers, like the priest and Rinaldi, Henry feels that the war is over for him. "It was not my show anymore," he ruminates. Soon, though, the needs of his body distract him from these thoughts. He needs to eat, drink, and sleep with Catherine, whom he dreams of taking away to a safe place.

ANALYSIS: CHAPTERS XXX–XXXII

In these last chapters of Book Three, the already delicate world of the Italian military falls apart. This unraveling begins in Chapter XXIX with the crumbling of Henry's normally calm exterior, which leads him to shoot the engineering sergeant. The world descends even further into chaos: the panicky Italian rear guard begins shooting at its own men; Bonello, fearing death, abandons Henry and Piani; and the neat columns that characterized the retreat at its beginning have broken into a terrifying mob. Battle police randomly pull officers from the columns of retreating men and execute them on sight. Hemingway expertly evokes the horror, confusion, and irrationality of war.

Chapter XXX presents two types of characters as a counterpoint to Henry. The zealous patriotism of the moblike battle police stands in contrast to Henry's distrust of noble ideals. Their rhetoric of God, blood, and soil, in its senselessness and cruelty, makes Henry's skepticism appear saintly. The character of the officer who is executed is more complex. The grim and sobering tone of his question—"Have you ever been in a retreat?"—resonates with Henry's realistic outlook. The officer, however, is resigned to his defeat. He neither flees nor protests his execution. Still, he tries to salvage a quiet dignity by asking not to be pestered with stupid questions before he is shot. Henry, however, is neither defeated nor interested in saving face. Because he doesn't believe in the sacredness of war or victory, he cannot muster a response comparable to the officer's. He flees not out of cowardice but out of an unwillingness to make a sacrifice for a cause that, to him, seems meaningless. In the context of total irrationality, self-preservation seems to him as valid a choice as any.

Just as war has been stripped of its romantic ideals, Henry strips himself of the stars that mark him as a lieutenant. With this action, he feels as if a certain portion of his life is over. His escape through the river is a baptism of sorts, a journey that washes away his anger and obligations and renews his sense of what truly matters in the world. His thoughts return to Catherine. In these chapters, Henry makes a "separate peace," as he later calls it, with the war—the farewell to arms that gives the novel its title (Chapter XXXIV).

When Henry reflects on his farewell in Chapter XXXII, the narrative switches from the first person to the second. This shift doesn't mark the first time that Hemingway uses the second person, but it brings about the most extended usage of it in the text. Here, as in its earlier occurrences, the second person affects a colloquial, storytelling tone. More important, it asks the reader to identify with Henry and get inside his head. This device, which Hemingway reserves for Henry's more philosophical moments, is as startling as it is engaging. The repeated "you" jumps out of a text that has used "I" fairly consistently. To heighten the reader's sense of being inside Henry's head, Hemingway lets slide conventional rules of grammar and style. Semicolons proliferate and sentence fragments are strung together. Even after the narrative returns to the first person, this stream-of-consciousness style intensifies. Hunger intrudes upon Henry's thoughts about his presumed death and the welfare of his friends, and the narrative follows Henry as he drifts off to sleep with the diffuse sentence, "There were many places."

Chapters XXXIII–XXXVII

Summary: Chapter XXXIII
Henry gets off the train when it enters Milan. He goes to a wine shop and has a cup of coffee. The proprietor offers to help him, but Henry assures the man that he is in no trouble. After they share a glass of wine, Henry goes to the hospital, where he learns from the porter that Catherine has left for Stresa. He goes to visit Ralph Simmons, one of the opera singers that he encounters earlier, and asks about the procedures for traveling to Switzerland. Simmons, offering whatever help he can, gives Henry a suit of civilian clothes and sends him off to Stresa with best wishes.

Summary: Chapter XXXIV
Henry takes the train to Stresa. He feels odd in his new clothes, noticing the scornful looks that he receives as a young civilian. Still, he claims that such looks do not bother him, for he has made a "separate peace" with the war. The train arrives in Stresa, and Henry heads for a hotel called the Isles Borromées. He takes a nice

room and tells the concierge that he is expecting his wife. In the bar, Emilio, the bartender, reports that he has seen two English nurses staying at a small hotel near the train station. Henry eats but does not answer Emilio's questions about the war, which, he reflects, is over for him.

Catherine and Helen Ferguson are having supper when Henry arrives at their hotel. While Catherine is overjoyed, Helen becomes angry and berates Henry for making such a mess of her friend's life. Neither Henry nor Catherine yields to Helen's stern moralizing, and soon Helen begins to cry. Henry describes the night spent with Catherine: he has returned to a state of bliss, though his thoughts are darkened by the knowledge that the "world breaks everyone" and that good people die "impartially."

In the morning, Henry refuses the newspaper, and Catherine asks if his experience was so bad that he cannot bear to read about it. He promises to tell her about it someday if he ever gets "it straight in [his] head." He admits to feeling like a criminal for abandoning the army, but Catherine jokingly assures him that he is no criminal: after all, she says, it was only the *Italian* army. They agree that taking off for Switzerland would be lovely, and return to bed.

SUMMARY: CHAPTER XXXV

Later that morning, Catherine goes to see Helen, and Henry goes fishing with Emilio. Emilio offers to lend Henry his boat at any time. Henry and Catherine eat lunch with Helen Ferguson. Count Greffi, a ninety-four-year-old nobleman whom Henry befriends on an earlier trip to Stresa, is also at the hotel with his niece. That evening, Henry plays billiards with the count. They talk about how the count mistakenly thought religious devotion would come with age and about whether Italy will win the war.

SUMMARY: CHAPTER XXXVI

Later that night, Emilio wakes Henry to inform him that the military police plan to arrest Henry in the morning. He suggests that Henry and Catherine row to Switzerland. Henry wakes Catherine, and they pack and head down to the dock. Emilio stocks them up with brandy and sandwiches and lets them take the boat. He takes fifty lire for the provisions and tells Henry to send him five hundred francs for the boat after he is established in Switzerland.

SUMMARY: CHAPTER XXXVII

Because of a storm, the waters are choppy and rough. Henry rows all night, until his hands are dull with pain. Catherine takes a short turn rowing, then Henry resumes. Hours later, having stayed safely out of sight of customs guards, the couple lands in Switzerland. They eat breakfast, and, as expected, the Swiss guards arrest them and take them to Locarno, where they receive provisional visas to remain in Switzerland. The guards argue comically over where the couple will find the best winter sports. Relieved but tired, Catherine and Henry go to a hotel and immediately fall asleep.

ANALYSIS: CHAPTERS XXXIII–XXXVII

Up to this point in the novel, reactions to the war have been voiced primarily by those involved in it: officers, soldiers, nurses, and surgeons. When Henry flees the front line, his travels expose him to several civilian characters whose respective attitudes toward the war echo those of military personnel. Neither Simmons, Emilio, nor Count Greffi support the war, with Simmons and Emilio going so far as to help Henry escape from duty. This rather one-sided presentation of the public's perception of war advances the novel's fundamental argument that war offers more opportunities for senseless loss and destruction than for glory and honor.

As if to underline this point, Hemingway skewers a more optimistic contemporary of his during Henry's conversation with Count Greffi. Asked by Henry about literature written in wartime, the count names Henri Barbusse, author of the 1916 war novel *Le Feu* (*Under Fire*), and H. G. Wells, the English writer most famous for *The Island of Doctor Moreau* and *The War of the Worlds*. Wells also penned *Mr. Britling Sees It Through,* which the count mistakenly calls *Mr. Britling Sees Through It.* Hemingway, probably irritated by this book's upbeat take on the war, deflates the optimism of the work's title with Henry's rejoinder, "No, he doesn't." Henry's comment that he has read "nothing any good" makes clear that Hemingway dislikes Barbusse as well. Barbusse argues against the war in *Le Feu,* but the novel's collective, everyman perspective clashes with Hemingway's rugged individualism. (Barbusse's later devotion to the Communist Party and Stalin didn't win him many points with Hemingway either.) Beyond their disputatious nature, these literary inside jokes reinforce the sense of impending doom: the optimistic war novel winds up in the hands of wounded soldiers, and the grim reality of the war belies Wells's optimistic depiction.

Once reunited with Catherine, Henry seems content with his decision to abandon the military. Several times, he assures himself that he is done with the war, but his "separate peace" is, perhaps, more a matter of wishful thinking than an actual state of mind. Henry admits that his thoughts are muddled when it comes to the war and his role in it. He tells Catherine that he will one day share his experience, if he can "get it straight in [his] head." This psychological turmoil and Henry's declaration that he feels like a criminal for leaving the front speak to a conflict deeper than Henry is willing to admit.

As Catherine and Henry prepare to journey to Switzerland, there is a gathering sense of doom. Although Hemingway prizes sharp-edged realism too highly to rely on traditional means of foreshadowing, he manages to forecast the coming tragedy in a number of ways. Helen Ferguson's uncharacteristic outburst in the hotel points not so much to an extreme adherence to social mores or her fear of solitude as it does to an unspeakable sense that the world is a harmful place in which a love as true as Catherine and Henry's cannot survive. Henry's nighttime meditation—one of the most beautifully written and moving passages in the novel—echoes this sentiment. While his incredibly bleak observation that the world was designed to kill the good, the gentle, and the brave seems to come out of nowhere, it anticipates the workings of the cruel world that soon "break[s]" what he holds most dear.

CHAPTERS XXXVIII–XLI

SUMMARY: CHAPTER XXXVIII

By fall, Henry and Catherine have moved to a wooden house on a mountain outside the village of Montreux. They pass a splendid life together, enjoying the company of Mr. Guttingen and his wife, who live downstairs, and taking frequent walks into the peaceful nearby villages. One day, after Catherine has her hair done in town, the couple goes out for a beer, which Catherine believes will help keep the baby small. Catherine has been increasingly worried about the baby's size, since the doctor has warned her that she has a narrow pelvis. Again, Henry and Catherine discuss marriage. Catherine agrees to marry someday because it will make the child "legitimate," but she prefers to talk about the sights that she hopes to see, such as Niagara Falls and the Golden Gate Bridge, when the marriage makes her an American.

Three days before Christmas, snow falls. Catherine asks Henry if he feels restless. He says no, though he does wonder about Rinaldi, the priest, and the men on the front. Catherine, suspecting that Henry might be restless, suggests that he change something to reinvigorate his life. He agrees to grow a beard. Catherine suggests that she cut her hair to make her look more like Henry, but Henry doesn't like this idea. When she proposes that they try to fall asleep together at the same time, Henry is unable to and lies awake looking at Catherine and thinking for a long time.

SUMMARY: CHAPTER XXXIX

By mid-January, Henry's beard has come in fully. While out on a walk, he and Catherine stop at a dark, smoky inn. They relish their isolation and wonder if things will be spoiled when the "little brat" comes. Catherine says that she will cut her hair when she is thin again after the baby is born so that she can be "exciting" and Henry can fall in love with her all over again. He tells her that he loves her enough now and asks, "What do you want to do? Ruin me?"

SUMMARY: CHAPTER XL

In March, the couple moves to the town of Lausanne to be nearer to the hospital. They stay in a hotel there for three weeks. Catherine buys baby clothes, Henry exercises in the gym, and both feel that the baby will come soon and that therefore they should not lose any time together.

SUMMARY: CHAPTER XLI

Around three o'clock one morning, Catherine goes into labor. Henry takes her to the hospital, where she is given a nightgown and a room. She encourages Henry to go out for breakfast, which he does. When he returns to the hospital, he finds that Catherine has been taken to the delivery room. He goes in to see her; the doctor stands by as Catherine inhales an anesthetic gas to get her through the painful contractions. Later that afternoon, when Henry returns from lunch, Catherine has become intoxicated from the gas and has made little progress in her labor. The doctor tells Henry that the best solution would be a Caesarean operation. Catherine suffers unbearable pain and pleads for more gas. Finally, they wheel her out on a stretcher to perform the operation. Henry watches the rain outside.

The doctor soon comes out with a baby boy, for whom Henry, strangely, has no feelings. Henry sees the doctor fussing over the child, but he rushes off to see Catherine without speaking to him.

When Catherine asks about their son, Henry tells her that he is fine. The nurse gives him a quizzical look; ushering him outside, the nurse explains that the umbilical cord had strangled the child prior to birth.

Henry goes out for dinner. When he returns, the nurse tells him that Catherine is hemorrhaging. He is terrified that she will die. When he is finally allowed to see her, she tells him that she will die and asks him not to say the things that he once said to her to other girls. He stays with her until she dies. Once she is dead, he attempts to say goodbye but cannot find the sense in doing so. He leaves the hospital and walks back to his hotel in the rain.

ANALYSIS: CHAPTERS XXXVIII–XLI

Henry and Catherine's simple domestic rituals in the first half of this section illustrate their happiness together. Hemingway efficiently marks their distance from the outside world by juxtaposing this bliss, in Chapter XL, with news of the German attack: "It was March, 1918, and the German offensive had started in France. I drank whiskey and soda while Catherine unpacked and moved around the room." A subtle nervousness, however, hangs over the tranquility. Henry, as is typical for Hemingway's heroes, craves adventure and finds himself becoming restless with what has essentially become married life. When he shadowboxes at the gym, he can't bear to look at himself long in the mirror because a boxer with a beard looks strange to him. This clash of new and old identities explodes later when Henry feels nothing for his son. As much as Henry has desired his isolation from the world and solitude with Catherine, their exclusive union poses for him a new problem of maintaining a modicum of independence. While Catherine is happy to have their lives "all mixed up," Henry confesses, "I haven't any life at all any more." As the ending of the novel shows, Henry is still very much in love with Catherine. But when Catherine wants to make love, Henry wants to play chess. Love, the last ideal left standing in the novel, proves to be problematic, like glory and honor.

Throughout this last book, Hemingway foreshadows Catherine's death. Her attempt to keep the baby small by drinking beer anticipates the painful labor through which she will suffer, while her claim that the world has "broken" her echoes the passage in which Henry fears the death of the good and the gentle. These subtleties create an expectation that casts a pall on the domestic satisfaction and relative optimism that Catherine and Henry feel. When Catherine's death comes, Henry reports it in the baldest, most unadorned terms: "It seems she had one hemorrhage after another. They couldn't stop it. I went into the room and stayed with Catherine until she died." Although Hemingway shows only the tip of the iceberg, the reader feels the immeasurable grief that extends below the surface. Here, in its ability to evoke so much by using so little, is the power of Hemingway's writing.

Though the novel ends in tragedy, Catherine's death fails to initiate an epiphany in Henry. Her death is not the catalyst for a great change or revelation. The realization that *does* come only confirms the novel's largest thematic focus: both love and war lead to losses for which there is no compensation. The storm with which the novel ends reminds the reader of Catherine's fear of rain. In Chapter XIX, Catherine speaks about an unidentifiable malevolence in the world. The rain that now falls on Henry as he leaves the hospital signals the same destructive forces—forces that render one powerless, speechless, and hopeless. By ending on this note, the novel seems to suggest that any epiphany Henry might have had, any thoughts that might have given him a more promising perspective, or any words that might have lent him solace would be false or impossible. They belong to the realm of Rinaldi's prostitutes, of Henry's drinking, of Catherine's lust for love: each of these provides much needed shelter from the world's inhospitable forces. But, as the closing passage of *A Farewell to Arms* makes heartbreakingly clear, such shelter is always temporary.

IMPORTANT QUOTATIONS EXPLAINED

1. "There, darling. Now you're all clean inside and out. Tell
    me. How many people have you ever loved?"
        "Nobody."
        "Not even me?"
        "Yes, you."
        "How many others really?"
        "None."
        "How many have you—how do you say it?—stayed
    with?"
        "None."
        "You're lying to me."
        "Yes."
        "It's all right. Keep right on lying to me. That's what I
    want you to do. Were they pretty?"

Soon after Henry arrives at the American hospital in Milan, his relationship with Catherine Barkley becomes passionate. Initially a
means of alleviating the pain of war and private grief, their affair
continues to serve the very practical purpose of masking life's difficulties. As this passage from Chapter XVI illustrates, their game of
love distracts them from unpleasant circumstances—here, a procedure wherein Catherine "cleans out" Henry's insides to prepare him
for his operation. Indeed, Hemingway washes over the details of the
procedure by having Catherine say, "There, darling. Now you're
all clean inside and out." At this point, however, the couple's game,
though acknowledged by Catherine as a lie, is becoming more complicated. The reader is unsure of the depth of feeling that inspires
Henry's declaration of love and his honesty about sleeping with
other women. This dialogue establishes the importance of illusion
in Catherine and Henry's budding relationship.

2. I had seen nothing sacred, and the things that were glorious
    had no glory and the sacrifices were like the stockyards
    at Chicago if nothing was done with the meat except to
    bury it. There were many words that you could not stand
    to hear and finally only the names of places had dignity.
    Certain numbers were the same way and certain dates
    and these with the names of the places were all you could
    say and have them mean anything. Abstract words such
    as glory, honor, courage, or hallow were obscene beside
    the concrete names of villages, the numbers of roads, the
    names of rivers, the numbers of regiments and the dates.

When Henry meets the young patriot, Gino, on the ruined Bainsizza in Chapter XXVII, the two have a conversation that confirms
Henry's ambivalence about war. Gino prattles on about the sacredness of the fatherland and his own willingness to die for his country.
To Henry, such abstractions as honor, glory, and sacrifice do little to
explain or assuage the unbelievable destruction that he sees around
him. What matters, he decides, are the names of villages and soldiers, the concrete facts of decimated walls and dead bodies. He
believes that in order to discuss the war honestly, one must dismiss
artificial concepts and deal with terms grounded in the reality of
the war. He tarnishes the romanticized ideal of the military hero by
equating the "sacrifices" of human lives in war with the slaughter
of livestock. He further compares romantic riffs about honor and
glory to burying meat in the ground. Nothing can be sustained or
nurtured by such pointlessness.

QUOTATIONS

3. When we were out past the tanneries onto the main road the troops, the motor trucks, the horse-drawn carts and the guns were in one wide slow-moving column. We moved slowly but steadily in the rain, the radiator cap of our car almost against the tailboard of a truck that was loaded high, the load covered with wet canvas. Then the truck stopped. The whole column was stopped. It started again and we went a little farther, then stopped. I got out and walked ahead, going between the trucks and carts and under the wet necks of the horses.

In this passage from Chapter XXVIII, Hemingway opens his description of the Italian army's retreat. The prose is indicative of Hemingway's style: bold, declarative sentences; a sharp eye for detail; and a rhythm that underscores the physical and emotional movement being described. Here, the rhythm of the two long opening sentences, which fluidly describe the great convergence and crawling pace of the retreating troops, is interrupted by short bursts that detail the action accurately. The repetition of "stopped" in "Then the truck stopped. The whole column stopped" jars the reader, as does the jerky motion of the subsequent "It started again . . . then stopped," brilliantly mimicking the stop-and-go action of the troops.

QUOTATIONS

4. But we were never lonely and never afraid when we were together. I know that the night is not the same as the day: that all things are different, that the things of the night cannot be explained in the day, because they do not then exist, and the night can be a dreadful time for lonely people once their loneliness has started. But with Catherine there was almost no difference in the night except that it was an even better time. If people bring so much courage to this world the world has to kill them to break them, so of course it kills them. The world breaks every one and afterward many are strong at the broken places. But those that will not break it kills. It kills the very good and the very gentle and the very brave impartially. If you are none of these you can be sure it will kill you too but there will be no special hurry.

These musings from Chapter XXXIV, when Henry lies in bed with Catherine after their reunion in Stresa, cast a long shadow from which the couple cannot escape. Henry's thoughts here are initially positive, focusing on how Catherine's presence alleviates his feelings of loneliness. He stresses an important aspect of their relationship: together, they manage to overcome the great sense of fear and loneliness that they feel in the presence of other people. Henry's rapturous thinking about Catherine, however, disconcertingly switches to a dark philosophy that maintains that the world was designed to kill the good, the gentle, and the brave—all terms that Henry has used or will use to describe Catherine. This unforced glide from contentedness into pessimism seems to reflect the inevitable inability of such positive forces as love to neutralize the grim reality of life. Indeed, from this point on, Henry and Catherine seem to be running from a force that means them harm and that, soon enough, catches up with them.

5. Poor, poor dear Cat. And this was the price you paid for sleeping together. This was the end of the trap. This was what people got for loving each other. Thank God for gas, anyway. What must it have been like before there were anesthetics?

Several times in the novel, as in this moment from the final chapter when Henry watches Catherine suffer through the agony of delivering their child, Henry performs the narrative equivalent of shaking his fist at the heavens and cursing the universe. This passage is significant for two reasons: first, it can be used to explain Hemingway's sometimes problematic treatment of the relationships between men and women. Hemingway tends to depict women as cold and domineering or as overly sweet and submissive. Some readers complain that Catherine falls into the second category. Henry's profound sense of loss and impotence—never welcomed among Hemingway's male characters—suggests that one of the motivations behind these somewhat stereotypical representations might be a belief that women possess an inherent "unmanly" helplessness.

The second facet of this quotation's significance lies in Henry's declaration, "Thank God for gas, anyway." Throughout the novel, characters have sought whatever means possible to shield themselves from the pain of the world. Rinaldi finds comfort in sex, the priest in God, Catherine and Henry in love, and almost everybody in alcohol. Each of these things acts as a form of anesthetic, a temporary dulling of a pain that, in the end, cannot be conquered.

QUOTATIONS

KEY FACTS

FULL TITLE
A Farewell to Arms

AUTHOR
Ernest Hemingway

TYPE OF WORK
Novel

GENRE
Literary war novel

LANGUAGE
English

TIME AND PLACE WRITTEN
1926–1928; America and abroad

DATE OF FIRST PUBLICATION
1929

PUBLISHER
Charles Scribner's Sons

NARRATOR
Lieutenant Frederic Henry

POINT OF VIEW
Henry narrates the story in the first person but sometimes
switches to the second person during his more philosophical
reflections. Henry relates only what he sees and does and
only what he could have learned of other characters from his
experiences with them.

TONE
As the autobiographical nature of the work suggests,
Hemingway's apparent attitude toward the story is identical to
that of the narrator.

TENSE
Past

SETTING (TIME)
1916–1918, in the middle of World War I

SETTING (PLACE)
Italy and Switzerland

PROTAGONIST
Frederic Henry

MAJOR CONFLICT
While there is no single, clear-cut conflict, friction does arise when Henry's love for Catherine cannot quell his innate restlessness.

RISING ACTION
Henry and Catherine's flirtatious games prepare and sometimes foreshadow their love for each other; their last days together before Henry's return to the front zero in on the demands of love versus Henry's life outside his relationship with Catherine.

CLIMAX
Broadly speaking, the Italian retreat, but more specifically, Henry's capture and near-execution by the battle police

FALLING ACTION
Henry's decision to flee and quit the army marks his farewell to arms and his commitment to Catherine.

THEMES
The grim reality of war, the relationship between love and pain, feelings of loss

MOTIFS
Masculinity, games and divertissement, loyalty versus abandonment, illusions and fantasies, alcoholism

SYMBOLS
While Hemingway avoids the sort of symbol that neatly equates an object with some lofty abstraction, he offers many powerfully evocative descriptions that often resonate with several meanings. Among these are the rain, which scares Catherine and into which Henry walks at the end of the novel;

KEY FACTS

Henry's description of her hair; the painted horse; and the
silhouette cutter Henry meets on the street.

FORESHADOWING

Catherine's conviction that dreadful things are going to occur;
the rainfall that scares her in the night; the doctor's warning
that Catherine's hips are narrow; Henry's musing on how life
kills the good, the gentle, and the brave

STUDY QUESTIONS

1.   A FAREWELL TO ARMS *is one of the most famous war*
     novels ever written. Unlike many war stories, however,
     the novel does not glorify the experience of combat
     or offer us portraits of heroes as they are traditionally
     conceived. What is the novel's attitude toward war? Is
     it fair to call A FAREWELL TO ARMS *an antiwar novel?*

As the title suggests, *A Farewell to Arms* is in many ways an an-
tiwar novel, but it would not be fair to connect this novel with a
literature of pacifism or social protest. In the novel's value system,
violence is not necessarily wrong—neither Henry nor Bonello feels
any remorse for shooting the engineering sergeant, and the reader
believes Henry when he tells Catherine that he will kill the police if
they come to arrest him. Furthermore, the novel glorifies discipline,
competence, and masculinity and portrays war as a setting in which
those qualities are constantly on display.

Nevertheless, *A Farewell to Arms* opposes the thoughtless violence, massive destruction, and sheer senselessness of war. It also
criticizes the psychological damage that war inflicts on individuals
and populations and its brutal upheaval of the lives of survivors.
In the face of such devastation, the novel posits, victory and defeat
are meaningless terms. Unlike many novels that glorify courage in
battle, *A Farewell to Arms* attempts to give a realistic portrayal of a
terrifying and, at the time of World War I, new kind of war. Never
before had men fought with machines and artillery capable of bringing about such annihilation. Still, the aim of the novel is not to protest war or encourage peace; it is simply to depict the hostility and
violence of a universe in which such a conflict is possible.

2.   *Discuss the various ways in which characters seek
     solace from the pains of a war-ravaged world. In the
     end, what does the novel suggest about such comforts?*

From the beginning of the novel, nearly every character has a habit to which he or she turns to help alleviate his or her private suffering. Mourning the death of her fiancé, Catherine plays a distracting game of seduction with Henry. Rinaldi loses himself in the comforts of women, while the priest uses his faith in God to ease the pain of the war and the ruthless taunting of the soldiers. Nearly all of the characters rely heavily on alcohol to numb the daily assaults of the war, both physical and emotional.

The most appealing of all of these comforts is love, which Hemingway explores for its power to endow characters with a sense of security. Upon meeting, Henry and Catherine imitate conventional courtship, speaking words that seem stolen from a scripted romance. They engage in such behavior, they admit, in order to take their minds off the war. As their love grows stronger and more legitimate, they continue to treat it as a protective shelter: Henry abandons the army and ends up living in the supposed safety of neutral Switzerland.

In the end, however, nothing offers lasting protection. Rinaldi, Henry suspects, has succumbed to syphilis, reflecting the degenerate nature of Rinaldi's values. The priest's philosophies regarding God are outdone by Henry's belief in the hollowness of lofty abstractions. Catherine, despite her all-consuming love, dies in childbirth. The novel suggests that no matter where characters turn for solace from the harsh circumstances of the world, the need for comfort and protection can never be fulfilled.

3. *Discuss Frederic Henry as a narrator. Assuming that, as a character, he is writing his story many years after living it, how does he convey its sense of extreme immediacy?*

The descriptive immediacy of *A Farewell to Arms* is the novel's most distinctive feature, and Hemingway achieves it through a simple, but expertly executed, technique: he allows Henry, as the narrator, to describe events according to his own perception and memories. The story never strays from Henry's vantage point. Even panoramic scenes of war and the afflicted Italian countryside, such as the passages describing the great retreat, are filtered through Henry's eyes—the reader sees only what Henry sees. Because Hemingway never offers objective narration (in which an omniscient, omnipresent voice tells the story), he must render the chaos and confusion and brutality of war by using only Henry's experiences. In choosing these experiences so skillfully, Hemingway is able to communicate the bleakness of one of the most traumatic times in world history—World War I—by focusing, for instance, on a conflict between two men: when Henry shoots the fleeing engineering sergeant, his actions convey the grim reality of a world that enables him to behave in such a way.

Additionally, the lack of other viewpoints contributes to the immediacy of the story—Henry, as though he is perpetually too engrossed in the moment to think outside of himself, never imagines the perceptions or feelings of other characters. He does not, for instance, presume to know what Catherine thinks or that she ever thinks anything other than what she says. Like a reporter, he simply reports what he sees and hears. This technique binds the reader to Henry's experience, and interpretation, of the events that he details.

How to Write
Literary Analysis

The Literary Essay: A Step-by-Step Guide

When you read for pleasure, your only goal is enjoyment. You might find yourself reading to get caught up in an exciting story, to learn about an interesting time or place, or just to pass time. Maybe you're looking for inspiration, guidance, or a reflection of your own life. There are as many different, valid ways of reading a book as there are books in the world.

When you read a work of literature in an English class, however, you're being asked to read in a special way: you're being asked to perform *literary analysis*. To analyze something means to break it down into smaller parts and then examine how those parts work, both individually and together. Literary analysis involves examining all the parts of a novel, play, short story, or poem—elements such as character, setting, tone, and imagery—and thinking about how the author uses those elements to create certain effects.

A literary essay isn't a book review: you're not being asked whether or not you liked a book or whether you'd recommend it to another reader. A literary essay also isn't like the kind of book report you wrote when you were younger, where your teacher wanted you to summarize the book's action. A high school- or college-level literary essay asks, "How does this piece of literature actually work?" "How does it do what it does?" and, "Why might the author have made the choices he or she did?"

The Seven Steps
No one is born knowing how to analyze literature; it's a skill you learn and a process you can master. As you gain more practice with this kind of thinking and writing, you'll be able to craft a method that works best for you. But until then, here are seven basic steps to writing a well-constructed literary essay:

1. Ask questions
2. Collect evidence
3. Construct a thesis

4. *Develop and organize arguments*
5. *Write the introduction*
6. *Write the body paragraphs*
7. *Write the conclusion*

---

1. ASK QUESTIONS

When you're assigned a literary essay in class, your teacher will often provide you with a list of writing prompts. Lucky you! Now all you have to do is choose one. Do yourself a favor and pick a topic that interests you. You'll have a much better (not to mention easier) time if you start off with something you enjoy thinking about. If you are asked to come up with a topic by yourself, though, you might start to feel a little panicked. Maybe you have too many ideas—or none at all. Don't worry. Take a deep breath and start by asking yourself these questions:

- **What struck you?** Did a particular image, line, or scene linger in your mind for a long time? If it fascinated you, chances are you can draw on it to write a fascinating essay.

- **What confused you?** Maybe you were surprised to see a character act in a certain way, or maybe you didn't understand why the book ended the way it did. Confusing moments in a work of literature are like a loose thread in a sweater: if you pull on it, you can unravel the entire thing. Ask yourself why the author chose to write about that character or scene the way he or she did and you might tap into some important insights about the work as a whole.

- **Did you notice any patterns?** Is there a phrase that the main character uses constantly or an image that repeats throughout the book? If you can figure out how that pattern weaves through the work and what the significance of that pattern is, you've almost got your entire essay mapped out.

- **Did you notice any contradictions or ironies?** Great works of literature are complex; great literary essays recognize and explain those complexities. Maybe the title (*Happy Days*) totally disagrees with the book's subject matter (hungry orphans dying in the woods). Maybe the main character acts one way around his family and a completely different way around his friends and associates. If you can find a way to explain a work's contradictory elements, you've got the seeds of a great essay.

At this point, you don't need to know exactly what you're going to say about your topic; you just need a place to begin your exploration. You can help direct your reading and brainstorming by formulating your topic as a *question,* which you'll then try to answer in your essay. The best questions invite critical debates and discussions, not just a rehashing of the summary. Remember, you're looking for something you can *prove or argue* based on evidence you find in the text. Finally, remember to keep the scope of your question in mind: is this a topic you can adequately address within the word or page limit you've been given? Conversely, is this a topic big enough to fill the required length?

Good Questions

> *"Are Romeo and Juliet's parents responsible for the deaths of their children?"*
> *"Why do pigs keep showing up in* Lord of the Flies?*"*
> *"Are Dr. Frankenstein and his monster alike? How?"*

Bad Questions

> *"What happens to Scout in* To Kill a Mockingbird?*"*
> *"What do the other characters in* Julius Caesar *think about Caesar?"*
> *"How does Hester Prynne in* The Scarlet Letter *remind me of my sister?"*

---

2. Collect Evidence

Once you know what question you want to answer, it's time to scour the book for things that will help you answer the question. Don't worry if you don't know what you want to say yet—right now you're just collecting ideas and material and letting it all percolate. Keep track of passages, symbols, images, or scenes that deal with your topic. Eventually, you'll start making connections between these examples and your thesis will emerge.

Here's a brief summary of the various parts that compose each and every work of literature. These are the elements that you will analyze in your essay, and which you will offer as evidence to support your arguments. For more on the parts of literary works, see the Glossary of Literary Terms at the end of this section.

ELEMENTS OF STORY   These are the *what*s of the work—what happens, where it happens, and to whom it happens.

- **Plot:** All of the events and actions of the work.

- **Character:** The people who act and are acted upon in a literary work. The main character of a work is known as the *protagonist.*

- **Conflict:** The central tension in the work. In most cases, the protagonist wants something, while opposing forces (antagonists) hinder the protagonist's progress.

- **Setting:** When and where the work takes place. Elements of setting include location, time period, time of day, weather, social atmosphere, and economic conditions.

- **Narrator:** The person telling the story. The narrator may straightforwardly report what happens, convey the subjective opinions and perceptions of one or more characters, or provide commentary and opinion in his or her own voice.

- **Themes:** The main idea or message of the work—usually an abstract idea about people, society, or life in general. A work may have many themes, which may be in tension with one another.

ELEMENTS OF STYLE   These are the *how*s—how the characters speak, how the story is constructed, and how language is used throughout the work.

- **Structure and organization:** How the parts of the work are assembled. Some novels are narrated in a linear, chronological fashion, while others skip around in time. Some plays follow a traditional three- or five-act structure, while others are a series of loosely connected scenes. Some authors deliberately leave gaps in their works, leaving readers to puzzle out the missing information. A work's structure and organization can tell you a lot about the kind of message it wants to convey.

- **Point of view:** The perspective from which a story is told. In *first-person point of view,* the narrator involves him or herself in the story. ("I went to the store"; "We watched in horror as the bird slammed into the window.") A first-person narrator is usually the protagonist of the work, but not always. In *third-person point of view,* the narrator does not participate in the story. A third-person narrator may closely follow a specific character, recounting that individual character's thoughts or experiences, or it may be what we call an *omniscient* narrator. Omniscient narrators see and know all: they can witness any event in any time or place and are privy to the inner thoughts and feelings of all characters. Remember that the narrator and the author are not the same thing!

- **Diction:** Word choice. Whether a character uses dry, clinical language or flowery prose with lots of exclamation points can tell you a lot about his or her attitude and personality.

- **Syntax:** Word order and sentence construction. Syntax is a crucial part of establishing an author's narrative voice. Ernest Hemingway, for example, is known for writing in very short, straightforward sentences, while James Joyce characteristically wrote in long, incredibly complicated lines.

- **Tone:** The mood or feeling of the text. Diction and syntax often contribute to the tone of a work. A novel written in short, clipped sentences that use small, simple words might feel brusque, cold, or matter-of-fact.

- **Imagery:** Language that appeals to the senses, representing things that can be seen, smelled, heard, tasted, or touched.

- **Figurative language:** Language that is not meant to be interpreted literally. The most common types of figurative language are *metaphors* and *similes,* which compare two unlike things in order to suggest a similarity between them— for example, "All the world's a stage," or "The moon is like a ball of green cheese." (Metaphors say one thing *is* another thing; similes claim that one thing is *like* another thing.)

---

3. Construct a Thesis

When you've examined all the evidence you've collected and know how you want to answer the question, it's time to write your thesis statement. A *thesis* is a claim about a work of literature that needs to be supported by evidence and arguments. The thesis statement is the heart of the literary essay, and the bulk of your paper will be spent trying to prove this claim. A good thesis will be:

- **Arguable.** "*The Great Gatsby* describes New York society in the 1920s" isn't a thesis—it's a fact.

LITERARY ANALYSIS

- **Provable through textual evidence.** "*Hamlet* is a confusing but ultimately very well-written play" is a weak thesis because it offers the writer's personal opinion about the book. Yes, it's arguable, but it's not a claim that can be proved or supported with examples taken from the play itself.

- **Surprising.** "Both George and Lenny change a great deal in *Of Mice and Men*" is a weak thesis because it's obvious. A really strong thesis will argue for a reading of the text that is not immediately apparent.

- **Specific.** "Dr. Frankenstein's monster tells us a lot about the human condition" is *almost* a really great thesis statement, but it's still too vague. What does the writer mean by "a lot"? *How* does the monster tell us so much about the human condition?

GOOD THESIS STATEMENTS

Question: In *Romeo and Juliet*, which is more powerful in shaping the lovers' story: fate or foolishness?

Thesis: "Though Shakespeare defines Romeo and Juliet as 'star-crossed lovers' and images of stars and planets appear throughout the play, a closer examination of that celestial imagery reveals that the stars are merely witnesses to the characters' foolish activities and not the causes themselves."

Question: How does the bell jar function as a symbol in Sylvia Plath's *The Bell Jar*?

Thesis: "A bell jar is a bell-shaped glass that has three basic uses: to hold a specimen for observation, to contain gases, and to maintain a vacuum. The bell jar appears in each of these capacities in *The Bell Jar*, Plath's semi-autobiographical novel, and each appearances marks a different stage in Esther's mental breakdown."

Question: Would Piggy in *The Lord of the Flies* make a good island leader if he were given the chance?

Thesis: "Though the intelligent, rational, and innovative Piggy has the mental characteristics of a good leader, he ultimately lacks the social skills necessary to be an effective one. Golding emphasizes this point by giving Piggy a foil in the charismatic Jack, whose magnetic personality allows him to capture and wield power effectively, if not always wisely."

4. DEVELOP AND ORGANIZE ARGUMENTS

The reasons and examples that support your thesis will form the middle paragraphs of your essay. Since you can't really write your thesis statement until you know how you'll structure your argument, you'll probably end up working on steps 3 and 4 at the same time.

There's no single method of argumentation that will work in every context. One essay prompt might ask you to compare and contrast two characters, while another asks you to trace an image through a given work of literature. These questions require different kinds of answers and therefore different kinds of arguments. Below, we'll discuss three common kinds of essay prompts and some strategies for constructing a solid, well-argued case.

TYPES OF LITERARY ESSAYS

- **Compare and contrast**

  Compare and contrast the characters of Huck and Jim in THE ADVENTURES OF HUCKLEBERRY FINN.

  Chances are you've written this kind of essay before. In an academic literary context, you'll organize your arguments the same way you would in any other class. You can either go *subject by subject* or *point by point*. In the former, you'll discuss one character first and then the second. In the latter, you'll choose several traits (attitude toward life, social status, images and metaphors associated with the character) and devote a paragraph to each. You may want to use a mix of these two approaches—for example, you may want to spend a paragraph a piece broadly sketching Huck's and Jim's personalities before transitioning into a paragraph or two that describes a few key points of comparison. This can be a highly effective strategy if you want to make a counterintuitive argument—that, despite seeming to be totally different, the two objects being compared are actually similar in a very important way (or vice versa). Remember that your essay should reveal something fresh or unexpected about the text, so think beyond the obvious parallels and differences.

- **Trace**

  Choose an image—for example, birds, knives, or eyes—and trace that image throughout MACBETH.

  Sounds pretty easy, right? All you need to do is read the play, underline every appearance of a knife in *Macbeth,* and then list them in your essay in the order they appear, right? Well, not exactly. Your teacher doesn't want a simple catalog of examples. He or she wants to see you make *connections* between those examples—that's the difference between summarizing and analyzing. In the *Macbeth* example above, think about the different contexts in which knives appear in the play and to what effect. In *Macbeth*, there are real knives and imagined knives; knives that kill and knives that simply threaten. Categorize and classify your examples to give them some order. Finally, always keep the overall effect in mind. After you choose and analyze your examples, you should come to some greater understanding about the work, as well as your chosen image, symbol, or phrase's role in developing the major themes and stylistic strategies of that work.

- **Debate**

  Is the society depicted in 1984 good for its citizens?

  In this kind of essay, you're being asked to debate a moral, ethical, or aesthetic issue regarding the work. You might be asked to judge a character or group of characters (*Is Caesar responsible for his own demise?*) or the work itself (*Is* JANE EYRE *a feminist novel?*). For this kind of essay, there are two important points to keep in mind. First, don't simply base your arguments on your personal feelings and reactions. Every literary essay expects you to read and analyze the work, so search for evidence in the text. What do characters in *1984* have to say about the government of Oceania? What images does Orwell use that might give you a hint about his attitude toward the government? As in any debate, you also need to make sure that you define all the necessary terms before you begin to argue your case. What does it mean to be a "good" society? What makes a novel "feminist"? You should define your terms right up front, in the first paragraph after your introduction.

  Second, remember that strong literary essays make contrary and surprising arguments. Try to think outside the box. In the *1984* example above, it seems like the obvious answer would be no, the totalitarian society depicted in Orwell's novel is *not* good for its citizens. But can you think of any arguments for the opposite side? Even if your final assertion is that the novel depicts a cruel, repressive, and therefore harmful society, acknowledging and responding to the counterargument will strengthen your overall case.

5. WRITE THE INTRODUCTION

Your introduction sets up the entire essay. It's where you present your topic and articulate the particular issues and questions you'll be addressing. It's also where you, as the writer, introduce yourself to your readers. A persuasive literary essay immediately establishes its writer as a knowledgeable, authoritative figure.

An introduction can vary in length depending on the overall length of the essay, but in a traditional five-paragraph essay it should be no longer than one paragraph. However long it is, your introduction needs to:

- **Provide any necessary context.** Your introduction should situate the reader and let him or her know what to expect. What book are you discussing? Which characters? What topic will you be addressing?

- **Answer the "So what?" question.** Why is this topic important, and why is your particular position on the topic noteworthy? Ideally, your introduction should pique the reader's interest by suggesting how your argument is surprising or otherwise counterintuitive. Literary essays make unexpected connections and reveal less-than-obvious truths.

- **Present your thesis.** This usually happens at or very near the end of your introduction.

- **Indicate the shape of the essay to come.** Your reader should finish reading your introduction with a good sense of the scope of your essay as well as the path you'll take toward proving your thesis. You don't need to spell out every step, but you do need to suggest the organizational pattern you'll be using.

Your introduction should not:

- **Be vague.** Beware of the two killer words in literary analysis: *interesting* and *important*. Of course the work, question, or example is interesting and important—that's why you're writing about it!

- **Open with any grandiose assertions.** Many student readers think that beginning their essays with a flamboyant statement such as, "Since the dawn of time, writers have been fascinated with the topic of free will," makes them sound important and commanding. You know what? It actually sounds pretty amateurish.

- **Wildly praise the work.** Another typical mistake student writers make is extolling the work or author. Your teacher doesn't need to be told that "Shakespeare is perhaps the greatest writer in the English language." You can mention a work's reputation in passing—by referring to *The Adventures of Huckleberry Finn* as "Mark Twain's enduring classic," for example—but don't make a point of bringing it up unless that reputation is key to your argument.

- **Go off-topic.** Keep your introduction streamlined and to the point. Don't feel the need to throw in all kinds of bells and whistles in order to impress your reader—just get to the point as quickly as you can, without skimping on any of the required steps.

---

6. Write the Body Paragraphs

Once you've written your introduction, you'll take the arguments you developed in step 4 and turn them into your body paragraphs. The organization of this middle section of your essay will largely be determined by the argumentative strategy you use, but no matter how you arrange your thoughts, your body paragraphs need to do the following:

- **Begin with a strong topic sentence.** Topic sentences are like signs on a highway: they tell the reader where they are and where they're going. A good topic sentence not only alerts readers to what issue will be discussed in the following paragraph but also gives them a sense of what argument will be made *about* that issue. "Rumor and gossip play an important role in *The Crucible*" isn't a strong topic sentence because it doesn't tell us very much. "The community's constant gossiping creates an environment that allows false accusations to flourish" is a much stronger topic sentence— it not only tells us *what* the paragraph will discuss (gossip) but *how* the paragraph will discuss the topic (by showing how gossip creates a set of conditions that leads to the play's climactic action).

- **Fully and completely develop a single thought.** Don't skip around in your paragraph or try to stuff in too much material. Body paragraphs are like bricks: each individual

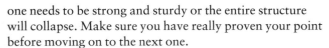

one needs to be strong and sturdy or the entire structure will collapse. Make sure you have really proven your point before moving on to the next one.

- **Use transitions effectively.** Good literary essay writers know that each paragraph must be clearly and strongly linked to the material around it. Think of each paragraph as a response to the one that precedes it. Use transition words and phrases such as *however, similarly, on the contrary, therefore,* and *furthermore* to indicate what kind of response you're making.

---

7. WRITE THE CONCLUSION

Just as you used the introduction to ground your readers in the topic before providing your thesis, you'll use the conclusion to quickly summarize the specifics learned thus far and then hint at the broader implications of your topic. A good conclusion will:

- **Do more than simply restate the thesis.** If your thesis argued that *The Catcher in the Rye* can be read as a Christian allegory, don't simply end your essay by saying, "And that is why *The Catcher in the Rye* can be read as a Christian allegory." If you've constructed your arguments well, this kind of statement will just be redundant.

- **Synthesize the arguments, not summarize them.** Similarly, don't repeat the details of your body paragraphs in your conclusion. The reader has already read your essay, and chances are it's not so long that they've forgotten all your points by now.

- **Revisit the "So what?" question.** In your introduction, you made a case for why your topic and position are important. You should close your essay with the same sort of gesture. What do your readers know now that they didn't know before? How will that knowledge help them better appreciate or understand the work overall?

- **Move from the specific to the general.** Your essay has most likely treated a very specific element of the work—a single character, a small set of images, or a particular passage. In your conclusion, try to show how this narrow discussion has wider implications for the work overall. If your essay on *To Kill a Mockingbird* focused on the character of Boo Radley, for example, you might want to include a bit in your conclusion about how he fits into the novel's larger message about childhood, innocence, or family life.

- **Stay relevant.** Your conclusion should suggest new directions of thought, but it shouldn't be treated as an opportunity to pad your essay with all the extra, interesting ideas you came up with during your brainstorming sessions but couldn't fit into the essay proper. Don't attempt to stuff in unrelated queries or too many abstract thoughts.

- **Avoid making overblown closing statements.** A conclusion should open up your highly specific, focused discussion, but it should do so without drawing a sweeping lesson about life or human nature. Making such observations may be part of the point of reading, but it's almost always a mistake in essays, where these observations tend to sound overly dramatic or simply silly.

A+ Essay Checklist

Congratulations! If you've followed all the steps we've outlined above, you should have a solid literary essay to show for all your efforts. What if you've got your sights set on an A+? To write the kind of superlative essay that will be rewarded with a perfect grade, keep the following rubric in mind. These are the qualities that teachers expect to see in a truly A+ essay. How does yours stack up?

- ✓ Demonstrates a thorough understanding of the book
- ✓ Presents an original, compelling argument
- ✓ Thoughtfully analyzes the text's formal elements
- ✓ Uses appropriate and insightful examples
- ✓ Structures ideas in a logical and progressive order
- ✓ Demonstrates a mastery of sentence construction, transitions, grammar, spelling, and word choice

Suggested Essay Topics

1. A FAREWELL TO ARMS *is a love story as well as a war novel. Discuss the role of love in the novel: how does love affect the characters' perceptions of war? How does the war shape the characters' love story?*

2. *F. Scott Fitzgerald considered Catherine's character the weak link in* A FAREWELL TO ARMS. *With attention to Catherine's values and motivations and to the way Hemingway portrays her character, do you agree with Fitzgerald's opinion? Why or why not?*

3. *What is the role of foreshadowing in* A FAREWELL TO ARMS? *How might Hemingway's subtle signaling to the reader that Catherine will die in childbirth change the way the reader approaches the final chapters?*

4. *Critics often discuss Hemingway's fiction as a celebration of a specific type of manhood. What kind of man does* A FAREWELL TO ARMS *celebrate, and how does Hemingway achieve this effect?*

A+ Student Essay

> Ernest Hemingway's *A Farewell to Arms* deals frankly
> and extensively with the sexual behavior of its principle
> characters. What role does sex play in the novel?

It would be easy to read *A Farewell to Arms* as a celebration of modern, freewheeling sexual liberation. For a book published in 1929, Hemingway's novel features a surprising amount of sexual activity as well as a plainspoken candor on the subject. Characters regularly visit brothels and talk and joke about sex, and the romance between the novel's narrator, Frederic Henry, and the nurse Catherine Barkley is grounded in their covert sexual relationship as much as anything else. However, a close examination reveals a more conflicted portrayal than we might first imagine. Hemingway clearly shows that his characters' sexual activities lead to profound negative consequences. In this way, he actually advances a relatively conservative view of sexual ethics, using the prevalence of casual, unmarried sex in the novel to demonstrate the terrible effects of wartime on the traditional moral order.

Throughout the novel, Frederic and his friends talk about sex and visit brothels in a strikingly casual way. For men in the military, this behavior is just part of daily life during wartime. Frederic's friend Rinaldi is probably the most appealing character in the whole book, and he also happens to be the most oversexed. He's a good doctor with a great sense of humor and a positive attitude, but he also has a penchant for drinking and prostitutes. Many of the other admirable characters in the book, such as Dr. Valentini, share Rinaldi's unsavory habits. Ironically, the characters portrayed most negatively, such as the pompous, abstemious war hero Ettore Moretti and the prudish head nurse Miss Van Campen, refrain from vices. In this way, Hemingway seems to prize certain characteristics (here, virility) that also predispose a man to certain weaknesses—at least during wartime, when marriage is impossible and there are special whorehouses set up for military officers. Nonetheless, Hemingway shows that moral vices can have dire consequences. In the end, Rinaldi contracts syphilis, a terrible disease that stems from his sexual behavior.

Frederic and Catherine's romance follows the same pattern: Their secret affair in the hospital seems exciting and attractive to the reader most of the time, but it eventually ends in disaster. In the final chapter, Catherine dies after giving birth to a stillborn child. Both her pregnancy and her death are clearly the result of her sexual relationship with Frederic. It would be simplistic to argue that Hemingway portrays Catherine's death as a just punishment for sexual indiscretion, but there *is* a moral element to the novel's grim conclusion. Catherine's demise is portrayed as the final act in a tragedy set against the disfigured moral landscape of wartime.

Catherine's relationship with Frederic is always placed in implicit contrast to her relationship with her fiancé, who died in France. Catherine and her fiancé were engaged for eight years but the couple remained chaste. (She explains this, somewhat obliquely, to Frederic in their first meeting). By comparison, Catherine and Frederic jump into a sexual relationship very quickly, sleeping together right after they are reunited in the hospital following Frederic's injury, and then postpone marriage indefinitely. Hemingway shows the ugly side of their affair when they spend a last night together in a sleazy hotel before he returns to the front. Catherine says she feels like a "whore," emphasizing how far their relationship in fact is from a normal courtship or marriage. In some regards, Catherine and Frederic's relationship functions exactly the way a good union between two people shouldn't, as the two grow increasingly isolated from society. They lose interest in their friends and promise they won't have to meet each other's parents. In the end, they flee to the total isolation of Switzerland. Instead of laying the foundation for a future life, surrounded by friends, family, and a supportive community—as in a good, traditional marriage—they cut themselves off from the world as much as possible.

In a broad sense, *A Farewell to Arms* is about the supreme difficulty of trying to live ethically in a situation—wartime—where the usual moral order has collapsed. During the Italian army's chaotic retreat, Frederic shoots an engineer who refuses to help with a vehicle, moments before Frederic himself abandons the same car. Later, he decides he can make a "separate peace" with war and abandon his post, implicitly asserting that his own conscience can trump the laws that ought to bind him to the army. But the episode with the engineer shows that, in a world that doesn't make sense, Frederic is morally adrift. Likewise, Frederic and Catherine try to have a romantic and sexual relationship outside of the normal moral framework of peacetime: marriage. Though their romance is beautifully and lyrically described, it ultimately leaves Catherine dead and, over its course, strips both of all their attachments to other people. Because the moral order is so upset by war, even good men, such as Rinaldi, and good relationships, such as Frederic and Catherine's, must end tragically.

GLOSSARY OF LITERARY TERMS

ANTAGONIST

The entity that acts to frustrate the goals of the *protagonist*. The antagonist is usually another *character* but may also be a non-human force.

ANTIHERO / ANTIHEROINE

A *protagonist* who is not admirable or who challenges notions of what should be considered admirable.

CHARACTER

A person, animal, or any other thing with a personality that appears in a *narrative*.

CLIMAX

The moment of greatest intensity in a text or the major turning point in the *plot*.

CONFLICT

The central struggle that moves the *plot* forward. The conflict can be the *protagonist's* struggle against fate, nature, society, or another person.

FIRST-PERSON POINT OF VIEW

A literary style in which the *narrator* tells the story from his or her own *point of view* and refers to himself or herself as "I." The narrator may be an active participant in the story or just an observer.

HERO / HEROINE

The principal *character* in a literary work or *narrative*.

IMAGERY

Language that brings to mind sense-impressions, representing things that can be seen, smelled, heard, tasted, or touched.

MOTIF

A recurring idea, structure, contrast, or device that develops or informs the major *themes* of a work of literature.

NARRATIVE

A story.

NARRATOR
The person (sometimes a *character*) who tells a story; the *voice* assumed by the writer. The narrator and the author of the work of literature are not the same person.

PLOT
The arrangement of the events in a story, including the sequence in which they are told, the relative emphasis they are given, and the causal connections between events.

POINT OF VIEW
The *perspective* that a *narrative* takes toward the events it describes.

PROTAGONIST
The main *character* around whom the story revolves.

SETTING
The location of a *narrative* in time and space. Setting creates mood or atmosphere.

SUBPLOT
A secondary *plot* that is of less importance to the overall story but may serve as a point of contrast or comparison to the main plot.

SYMBOL
An object, *character,* figure, or color that is used to represent an abstract idea or concept. Unlike an *emblem,* a symbol may have different meanings in different contexts.

SYNTAX
The way the words in a piece of writing are put together to form lines, phrases, or clauses; the basic structure of a piece of writing.

THEME
A fundamental and universal idea explored in a literary work.

TONE
The author's attitude toward the subject or *characters* of a story or poem or toward the reader.

VOICE
An author's individual way of using language to reflect his or her own personality and attitudes. An author communicates voice through *tone, diction,* and *syntax.*

LITERARY ANALYSIS

A NOTE ON PLAGIARISM

Plagiarism—presenting someone else's work as your own—rears its ugly head in many forms. Many students know that copying text without citing it is unacceptable. But some don't realize that even if you're not quoting directly, but instead are paraphrasing or summarizing, *it is plagiarism* unless you cite the source.

Here are the most common forms of plagiarism:

- Using an author's phrases, sentences, or paragraphs without citing the source
- Paraphrasing an author's ideas without citing the source
- Passing off another student's work as your own

How do you steer clear of plagiarism? You should *always* acknowledge all words and ideas that aren't your own by using quotation marks around verbatim text or citations like footnotes and endnotes to note another writer's ideas. For more information on how to give credit when credit is due, ask your teacher for guidance or visit www.sparknotes.com.

Review & Resources

Quiz

1. At the beginning of the novel, Henry reports that seven thousand soldiers have died due to what?

    A. Venereal disease
    B. The most recent enemy attack
    C. Cholera
    D. Starvation

2. Immediately before Henry kisses Catherine for the first time, they make a pact to do what?

    A. Keep their affair a secret from Rinaldi and Miss Ferguson
    B. Drop all discussion about the war
    C. Love each other always
    D. Meet the coming battle bravely

3. Hemingway famously said that a writer can "omit things that he knows and that a reader, if the writer is writing truly enough, will have a feeling of those things as strongly as though the writer had stated them." What term best describes this philosophy?

    A. The Iceberg Theory
    B. Unreliable Narration
    C. The Veil Theory
    D. The Objective Correlative

4. Before Henry heads off to the front at Pavla, what does Catherine give him?

    A. The toy riding crop once owned by her fiancé
    B. A bottle of grappa
    C. A love letter
    D. A St. Anthony medal

5. Before the trench mortar wounds him, why does Henry leave the dugout?

    A. To rescue one of his ambulance drivers who is stranded outside the dugout

    B. To get food for his drivers

    C. To prove to his men that he is brave

    D. He is about to abandon his troops but then changes his mind.

6. How does Mrs. Walker greet Henry upon his arrival at the American hospital in Milan?

    A. She tells him that she resents American boys fighting for foreign armies.

    B. She becomes frazzled because she cannot arrange a room for him without a doctor's orders.

    C. She sympathizes with him over his difficult train ride.

    D. She takes his temperature.

7. Why does the barber who comes to shave Henry almost kill him?

    A. He desperately wants to end the war and believes that killing an officer will make that happen.

    B. He mistakes Henry for an Austrian soldier.

    C. He is crazy.

    D. Henry resembles the man's son, who was killed earlier in the war.

8. What is the name of the good-natured doctor who agrees to operate on Henry's leg?

    A. Dr. Gorizia

    B. Dr. Influenza

    C. Dr. Pavla

    D. Dr. Valentini

9. Why does Catherine decide to bet on a certain horse in a race that she believes has been fixed?

   A. The horse limps.
   B. The horse has been dyed a different color.
   C. The horse is obviously much younger than the other horses.
   D. The horse has the best jockey.

10. How does Catherine respond to the news that Henry has received three weeks of convalescent leave?

    A. She tells him that she is pregnant.
    B. She screams that she never wants to see him again.
    C. She sobs for fear that he will lose his life if he returns to war.
    D. She seduces him and they make love.

11. What characteristic makes Ettore Moretti a good contrast to Lieutenant Henry?

    A. Ettore can sing.
    B. Ettore is an American.
    C. Ettore is a braggart.
    D. Ettore is an alcoholic.

12. What does Henry do when the engineering sergeants in Aymo's car refuse to help rescue the vehicle from the mud?

    A. He shrugs and lets them go.
    B. He orders Bonello and Aymo to beat them up.
    C. He shoots at them.
    D. He delivers a powerful speech about cowardice.

13. Where does Catherine accompany Henry before he leaves for the front?

    A. To the opera
    B. To a gun shop
    C. To a cathedral
    D. To the place where they met

14. In what year was *A Farewell to Arms* published?

    A. 1929
    B. 1918
    C. 1939
    D. 1953

15. Why do the battle police seize Henry?

    A. He is guilty of treason.
    B. He is an officer.
    C. He is suspected of killing Aymo.
    D. He trespassed at a local farmhouse.

16. How is Henry wounded after he crawls out of the river?

    A. The Italian rear guard shoots him.
    B. While crossing the great fields at Campoformio, he snags himself on a barbed wire fence.
    C. While attempting to hide on a train, he cuts his head.
    D. He falls down a rocky embankment.

17. In Milan, who lends Henry a suit of civilian clothing?

    A. A barkeep
    B. Ralph Simmons
    C. Rinaldi
    D. A farmer

18. What is Helen Ferguson's reaction upon seeing Henry in Stresa?

    A. She is overjoyed that he has kept his word and returned to Catherine.
    B. She is jealous of Catherine because she has long been in love with Henry.
    C. She is angry that he has complicated Catherine's life by seducing her and getting her pregnant.
    D. She is too concerned with her own problems to care much for Henry's return.

19. Why do the Swiss guards argue in front of Catherine and Henry?

   A. They disagree over what city offers the best winter sports.
   B. They are brothers and fight all the time.
   C. They do not agree on which procedure they should follow to process foreign visitors.
   D. They cannot decide whether or not to send the couple back to Italy.

20. Which destination do Catherine and Henry claim they have come to Switzerland to visit?

   A. Lucerne
   B. Murren
   C. Locarno
   D. Montreux

21. In later life, what nickname did Hemingway assume to convey a sense of strength, wisdom, and mastery?

   A. Sensei
   B. Top Cat
   C. Papa
   D. Big Kahuna

22. Why does Catherine suggest that Henry grow a beard?

   A. She fears that he is growing restless and needs a change.
   B. After all these months, he has grown ugly to her.
   C. It will help to disguise him in case the military police show up again.
   D. Having a beard will enable Henry to belong to the right social circles.

23. Before she dies, what does Catherine say that the world has done to her?

   A. That it has disappointed her
   B. That it makes her wish she had never been born
   C. That it has made her value true love
   D. That it has broken her

24. What place does Catherine dream of visiting after she officially marries Henry?

    A. Niagara Falls
    B. Paris
    C. Barcelona
    D. Los Angeles

25. What is Henry's reaction to his child's birth?

    A. He weeps with joy.
    B. He passes out cigars to the hospital staff.
    C. He shows no interest.
    D. He goes out for a drink.

ANSWER KEY

1: C; 2: B; 3: A; 4: D; 5: B; 6: B; 7: B; 8: D; 9: B; 10: A; 11: C; 12: C;
13: B; 14: A; 15: B; 16: C; 17: B; 18: C; 19: A; 20: A; 21: C; 22: A;
23: D; 24: A; 25: C

SUGGESTIONS FOR FURTHER READING

BLOOM, HAROLD. *Ernest Hemingway's* A FAREWELL TO ARMS. New York: Chelsea House Publishers, 1987.

DONALDSON, SCOTT, ed. *New Essays on* A FAREWELL TO ARMS. New York: Cambridge University Press, 1990.

GELLENS, JAY, ed. *Twentieth-Century Interpretations of* A FAREWELL TO ARMS: *A Collection of Critical Essays.* Englewood Cliffs, NJ: Prentice-Hall, 1970.

LEWIS, ROBERT W. A FAREWELL TO ARMS: *The War of the Words.* New York: Twayne Publishers, 1992.

MONTEIRO, GEORGE, ed. *Critical Essays on Ernest Hemingway's* A FAREWELL TO ARMS. New York: G. K. Hall & Co., 1994.

REYNOLDS, MICHAEL S. *Hemingway.* 5 vols. Detroit: Gale Group, 1998–2000.

WAGNER-MARTIN, LINDA. A FAREWELL TO ARMS: *A Reference Guide.* Westport, CT: Greenwood Press, 2003.

———, ed. *Ernest Hemingway: Seven Decades of Criticism.* East Lansing, MI: Michigan State University Press, 1998.